GRANDPA'S BOOK

GRANDPA'S BOOK

Raymond C. Fuller, Sr
(*Grandpa Ray*)
Edited by Millie Miner and Rose Phillips

Writers Club Press
San Jose New York Lincoln Shanghai

Grandpa's Book

Writers Club Press
an imprint of iUniverse.com, Inc.

For information address:
iUniverse.com, Inc.
5220 S 16th, Ste. 200
Lincoln, NE 68512
www.iuniverse.com

ISBN: 0-595-19957-7

Printed in the United States of America

Presented to

My Grandchildren

Matthew Raymond Fuller
David Kenneth Fuller
Katherine Elizabeth Fuller
Elizabeth Marie Young
Christopher Tomas Young
Lee James Gaiteri
Katrina Joy Gaiteri
Jessica Lynn Benedict
Jonathan Michael Benedict
Rebecca Marie Benedict
Samuel Carlos Benedict
Caleb Joseph Benedict
David Brian Goldberg, Jr.
Dominic Hickman
Thomas Leander Fuller
James Robert Fuller
William Francis Fuller
Grace Ann Fuller

My Children
Raymond Clarence Fuller, Jr.
Jacqueline Elizabeth Young
Terri Lee Gaiteri
Penny Sue Benedict
Pamela Jo Hickman
Thomas Willam Fuller

My Great Grandchildren
As of this date

Rachel Nicole Fuller

Introduction

I was eight years old in August of 1940 when my Grandfather, Thomas Leander Fuller, died at the age of 77. I have often wondered what my Grandfather's life was like. In the short span of time that I was able to share with him, I know that times were harsh and life was a struggle. I have wondered if my Grandfather had a sense of humor, what he did in his youth and early life. Frequently, I have wondered if he enjoyed some good times, excitement or genuine happiness. What tribulations, misfortunes and distress did he encounter? What was it like for him at the turn of the century from the 1800's to the 1900's? I will never know. Grandpa did leave several diaries but upon his death my Grandmother burned them. She felt that they were personal and didn't want anyone reading them. *Maybe, she had a special reason for burning them.*

Thomas Leander Fuller was born and raised in the Edmeston, NY area and lived his entire life there as did my father, Clarence. Thomas was born in Pittsfield, NY, a little community just four miles south of Edmeston. The only time that the family left Edmeston was in the year 1902-1903 when they moved to Lowville, NY, to be with their daughter Flossie Mai who was in a T.B. (tuberculosis) hospital where she died on January 4, 1903. Flossie would have been my aunt. My mother, Vera Welch Fuller, lost a sister, Kyra to the same dreaded disease before she met my father. Thus I lost two aunts to T.B. in the early part of the century.

"Grandpa's Book" is an attempt to give my Grandchildren something that they can look at in later years and hopefully enjoy, knowing what life was like in the 1930's the 1940's etc. and what their Grandfather did and how he lived. I have told the good and the bad, the humorous and the sad. I have tried to tell it like it was. Real life happenings with real life anecdotes that hopefully someday you will understand and maybe even relish.

I remember very little about my Grandfather. Most of you wouldn't know much about your Great Grandfather Clarence (my father) or your Great Grandmother Vera (my mother). My Grandfather seldom spoke. He was a quiet, kind and gentle man. My Grandmother, Vesta Green Fuller died in April, 1955 at the age of 83.

Keep **"Grandpa's Book"** for your old age. The pages may turn yellow but I think that you will enjoy it as you also become *"prehistoric."* I have included the Fuller Genealogy traced back to Dr. Samuel Fuller of the Mayflower. With this little book you have some idea how your Grandfather, Great Grandfather and your Great Great Grandfather lived. Things that mean little to you when you are young often become invaluable when you grow old. It is my hope that this little keepsake from your Grandfather might become, if not valuable, at least somewhat significant. Memories become more significant as we mature.

Grandpa Ray loves each one of you very much. My parents or my grandparents never told me that. *The Fuller Family* was never proficient at expressing their feelings. I know that they did love me but to actually say "*I love you*" has always been an uneasy thing for a Fuller to say.

"**Grandpa's Book**" is meant to be an expression of my love to my "most favorite people on earth"....my children, my grandchildren and my great grandchildren.

Grandpa Ray

ONE

On November 21, 1620 the now famous Mayflower ship
was headed for Virginia, but as a result of stormy weather
and navigational errors landed off coarse by about 500 miles.
It dropped anchor off the site of present day Provincetown
on the North end of Cape Cod, MA. On December 21,
1620 they disembarked near the head of
Cape Cod. (Present day Plymouth, MA).

Included on the ship with a crew of about
20 to 30 men were 102 "Pilgrims" of the Separatist
Congregation looking for religious freedom.
They were called Separatist because they
had split from the Church of England.
[They also are popularly referred to as Puritans.]

Among these courageous souls was their
one and only doctor, Dr. Samuel Fuller,
[the 8th Pilgrim to sign the Mayflower compact]
who was also a deacon in the Puritan Church.

His son, Samuel, became Reverend Samuel Fuller, a
minister in the Puritan movement. Somewhere along the
line, the Fullers turned to farming.

Today there are thousands of Dr. Fuller's
descendants living in the United States of America.

Dr. Fuller, my 8th great grandfather would probably look
on his many descendant with pride and delight.
Possibly in your Grandpa Ray's case "bewilderment."

Precisely 311 years and 11 days after Grandpa Sam and his
brother Edward Fuller set foot on Plymouth Rock and
ultimately upon American soil, I made my arrival known on
January 1, 1932. It was a cold, snowy winter afternoon.
Darkness was creeping in on the dairy farm located on a dirt
road about two miles north of the village of Edmeston, NY.

My father had cranked the handle on the wall mounted,
battery charged "New Lisbon" telephone that looked like a
box on the wall with a crank and a receiver and a mouth
piece. A wire ran from pole to pole, (or tree to tree) starting
in the village, to the farms on each road that had service and
then back to the village. Every farm that had phone service
was attached to the same wire. It was called a party line by
some, a gossip line by others, and to most folks it was
referred to as the rumor mill. Usually eight to ten neighbors
were on each line. When a person cranked the handle, every

one on the line heard the ringing and everyone listened in. Each subscriber had a different ring. For instance, we might have four short rings and the next door neighbor might need two long cranks of the handle. Everyone knew who was being called and everyone knew when you were calling out. Everyone knew that everyone else was listening. What else was there to do? Newspapers were often delivered a day late to the farms. There just was no better way of keeping up with the news and gossip.

When my father turned the handle on the phone, about eight to ten receivers were lifted so as to hear whatever news there might be to discover. The call was to Dr. Granger, "*the country doctor*," the kind of doctor that you have only heard about on TV or read about in books. He was more than a doctor to the people of Edmeston, he was their friend and caretaker. If you had no money (and many people didn't) it didn't matter to "Doc".... he was always there! He was often paid for his services with eggs, milk or meat, or a promise. Dr. Granger charged $1.00 for an office visit and $2.00 for a home visit. His accounts receivable book was as large as his heart. Some people didn't like "Old Doc" because he was a cigarette smoking, whiskey drinking man but some people are living today because of "Old Doc," including me. Dr. Granger came to Edmeston in 1926 and died with throat cancer in 1946. He had been known to charge as much as $25.00 for delivery of a baby before his death.

I don't remember very much about that first day. I only remember that I was cold and hungry. I came in both toothless and bald headed and it looks to me like that's the way I'm going to go out. They tell me that the doctor took me by the heels and turned me upside down and smacked me a real good one on the behind. This is how I started out in life, upside down and with a mistreated derriere. After the delivery, my father looked at the handsome little nursling and went to the barn to milk the cows. I was the 6th living child to be born into the family. One full term boy was stillborn late in 1919. One more, my sister, Barbara, would follow 3 years later to complete the family of 5 girls and 2 boys.

You have heard of the great depression of the 30's, well it started in 1929 and we were knee deep in the depression when I came along. Some mothers have been known to be depressed when a child was born, but in my case the whole country was depressed. My father used to say that he had always been so poor that he didn't even know that there was a depression. He just thought that he had caught up with the rest of the country. As it was, it was the other way around.

The Farm Home

The farm was a 200 acre family dairy farm supported by 25 to 30 milk cows and a few "dry and young stock." It also had a team of horses and between 200 to 300 egg laying hens and usually a couple of pigs. Other animals were introduced from time to time but, basically, it was cows and hens. There was no electricity, the toilet was an "*outhouse*" located at the far corner of the woodshed. The only so called "*running*" water for the house was a small pencil size trickle with absolutely no water pressure. Even though it took several minutes to fill a small pail, it was piped to the inside of the house and no one had to go out doors for water as did many of the farmers. The water was piped to the kitchen sink from a small spring north of the dairy barn. The water was first piped to a cement "*watering tub*" (a little bigger than a bath tub) for the animals and some was diverted to the house.

Historical note: Electric lights came to the village of Edmeston in 1925. In 1926 Schworms Store boasted of having an electric refrigerator. In 1927, Hopkins Hardware gave a demonstration of a radio at the Grange Hall. My father said that he ordered one that operated on the 32 volt batteries that could be generated by the Delco generator. Historians tell me that the Bank purchased a manual adding machine in 1929. In 1941 the REA announced plans and financing for installing electricity to the rural area. The war came in December and the plans were delayed until after the war.

My father had purchased a "Delco" generator that would run on a petroleum product (gasoline or kerosene) and it would generate enough electricity to charge a series of batteries (about 12) that were housed in the barn. These batteries were a little larger than a car battery but were made of glass and when fully charged would provide 32 volts of power. We used 25 watt light bulbs both in the house and in the barn. This was barely a little more light than a candle but to us it was electric and safe. It would power the radio that my father had purchased in 1927 and the short evenings were spent listening to that radio.

The Farm

We lived on that farm for my first 11 years so most of my early childhood memories are about the farm and farm life. When I refer to the big farm, this is the farm that I am talking about. Farm life was much different than it is today. Cows were milked by hand. Chickens were allowed to roam the chicken yard, and sometimes even the fields, to chase grasshoppers and whatever else they could find. Although we usually purchased 200 to 300 baby chickens in the early spring and put them in the brooder houses, some hens were allowed to hatch out their own baby chicks. I had a great fondness for ducks and, by the time I was 6 or 7, I was allowed to raise them from hatchlings. My father didn't particularly like them, as they would get into the cow's watering tub and make a real nasty mess, but I was allowed to keep them nevertheless.

Hay was brought into the barn on a horse drawn wagon, loose and not in bales as it is today. Corn was husked by hand and the kernels were removed by hand until my father bought a hand operated contraption that we called a "*Corn Sheller*." As we ran the corn through it, the cobs were stripped bare and the kernels fell into a bucket under the Corn Sheller. Our silos were filled with fodder corn that had been run through a chopper and blower. The silos were not much higher than the barn and in many cases not as high. Today, they are tall and look down on the barns and are often filled with grass ensilage. Oats and wheat were cut with a reap and binder that cut and tied it together in small bundles. It was then brought to the barn where a threshing machine would be set up to separate the oats or wheat from the straw. The straw was kept for the animals' bedding and the grain was placed in the granary. The farmers almost always worked together in groups helping each other to fill silos and to do the threshing.

Using a two-man crosscut saw to cut trees and a "*buzz saw*" to cut up the wood, my father and brother, Robert, would cut wood for the stoves from our own wood lot and, by the time I was 5 years old, I would help carry it into the woodshed and pile it up. I learned how to use an ax at a very early age as the wood had to be split for the kitchen stove. By the time I started school, filling the wood box by the kitchen stove was one of my everyday chores. On Saturdays, after cleaning the horse stalls, my sister, Pauline, and I used to take turns churning the butter in our big barrel butter churn. We had our own butter and buttermilk and my mother always made the worlds' greatest cottage cheese.

Since we had no refrigeration, ice was cut in the winter from a pond located on the south-end of the village of Edmeston. The ice pond was a source of income for John Burbon, the owner. It was cut into large rectangular pieces about two feet wide and three feet long and as deep as the pond had frozen, which was usually about two feet deep. It was hauled to our ice house by a horse drawn wagon or sleigh and packed in sawdust and it kept throughout the summer this way. We had what was called an ice box in the house to try to preserve food. Some of the ice was used in the ice box but mostly it was used in the milk house to cool the milk overnight as milk was only taken to the milk station in the village in the mornings.

Some men made most of their living hauling farmers' milk to the milk stations in milk cans that held forty quarts (eighty pounds) of milk. In our case, we paid a neighbor to haul our milk to the village. Each farmer was issued a number by the milk station and the number was painted onto the milk cans so that the milk station knew whose milk they were handling. The milk was weighed and tested for butter fat at the milk station and the farmers were paid accordingly.

I think that every farmer had a mortgage on their farm and on their animals. The first National Bank of Edmeston was usually the mortgage holder but I.T. & C.A. (Ike and Clayton) Welch (my Grandfather Mark Welch's cousins) often held the farm mortgage and the chattel on the livestock. It was customary for the milk company that bought the milk to withhold 1/3rd of the milk check to cover the payments. At times the feed store shared in the withholding. In the 1930's, farmers received their milk checks once a month on the 25th. I recall my father looking at his check, one day in the 1930's, and remarking to my mother that it wouldn't be hard to remember how much he had received as he had a check in the amount of $25.00 on the 25th. He was doing okay. The mortgage was paid, the feed store had its money, the cattle dealers had theirs and we had $25.00 for the month to feed and clothe seven kids. With the egg money coming in (perhaps another $10.00 or $15.00) and the fact that we raised almost all of our food, the family could be considered quite prosperous for this period of time. Many people were standing in long lines, hoping to receive a loaf of bread or a little soup.

Pigs were raised for food and chickens that failed to lay eggs regularly were great for Sunday dinners. A bull calf was often raised for veal and our beef usually came from cows that were no longer productive. Usually, we had plenty to eat, even during the depression, but there were times that food ran low and we found brown sugar in our sandwiches for our school lunch but that was very rare. *Not rare enough*! Bread was baked almost daily as was usually a cake or pie for dessert. A huge pan of potatoes was boiled for noon dinner and the leftovers were cooked up for supper, either fried or mixed with a white sauce. My father, like most farmers, almost never ate breakfast without fried potatoes, bacon and eggs or pancakes and sausages, often with oatmeal as a cereal.

My mother canned almost everything. The cellar was lined with canning jars. Very little was purchased from the grocery store. The exception being sugar, coffee, tea, crackers and other things that we couldn't raise on the farm or that my mother couldn't bake. Flour for baking was purchased in 50 or 100 pound bags as my mother made everything from scratch: bread, cookies, pies, cakes, rolls etc.

The fall was canning time and the garden yielded almost everything that we were going to eat for the next year including tomatoes, carrots, peas, just about every vegetable, along with fruit, that was usually purchased, except for apples and cherries. We had two nice cherry trees next to the house and my mother would try to beat the birds to the cherries so that she could bake cherry pies and can some of them. Our apple orchard was behind a field near the woods. The trees were never sprayed for insects so we just naturally expected to find a worm in any apple that we ate. We just learned to eat around them. This never really bothered us. What did bother us was when we would bite into an apple and find only half a worm. Some of the apples were made into applesauce and canned and others were pressed into cider and kept in a big wooden barrel to mature into cider vinegar. However, before it became vinegar it would become what is known as "hard cider" (usually much more intoxicating than beer), which would then, later turn into apple cider vinegar. Cabbage was chopped and placed into a crock and left to "*work*" until it turned into praiseworthy sauerkraut. Cucumbers were made into exceptional pickles.

Since we had no refrigeration, hogs were salted in a brine and placed in a crock to cure as hams and bacon. When a cow was butchered we ate fresh liver on butchering day. The tongue and heart was pickled and canned and, for the most part, the beef was cut up and canned in Mason canning jars. In the winter, meat could be preserved for short periods of time but it was usually cooked and canned right away. Usually a front quarter was treated with a salt brine and dried for dried beef. We didn't have a smoke house. Very often half of the cow or pig would be sold, since half a beef or pig was about all anyone could handle at a time without refrigeration. For several days after a hog was butchered, the house smelled of pork fat being rendered down into lard which was stored in a crock and used for baking and frying. All the pies, cakes and doughnuts were made with lard.

The creek that runs through the village of Edmeston from north to south known as Mill Creek, had a dam at both ends of the village. The dam at the northern end of the village [known as Ackerman's Dam] powered a mill, known as Ackerman's Mill, that manufactured sashes, blinds, doors, and moldings. I'll tell you more about the village and some of the people later.

The old timers tell me that at one time there were four or more dams on Mill Creek. I only remember two. The dam at the South end of town powered a grist mill that was run by John Burbon. This is where we got our ice in the winter and where I can recall going with my father to the grist mill and having our buckwheat ground into flour for my mother to make buckwheat pancakes. Old John Bourbon, the owner, died around 1939 and the mill was closed and left to rot on its foundation. The oats and wheat were usually taken to the feed store, run by the Talbot family, and ground and mixed for cattle grain or chicken mash and the dry corn was usually cracked (ground into small pieces) for the chickens.

March was sugaring season. Our woods included several maple trees. My father would tap the maple trees on the side of the trees facing south, by using a bit and auger to drill into the tree, and a metal spout was inserted and a pail hung on it to catch the sap. We didn't have a sugar house so we boiled our sap outdoors in a huge pan. Our neighbor did have a sugar house and at times my father did mix our sap with his and they would boil sap day and night until the end of the season. We always had plenty of home made maple syrup. Sometimes a small amount of the syrup would be boiled down to make maple sugar candy. However, usually if any candy was made it was made with molasses and that would be at Christmas time.

In the spring, my father would harness up the team of horses and start spring plowing. After plowing, he would drag the fields and plant the corn with a corn planter and the oats and wheat with a grain drill. The potatoes were planted by hand along with the big garden of every vegetable that we were going to eat in the summer, fall and the coming winter. Everything, except the oats and wheat, had to be continually cultivated to keep down the weeds. In June the horses were hitched to the mowing machine. It was time to start cutting the hay. After the sun dried the hay, he would rake it with a horse drawn dump rake. It was then *"bunched up"* into piles with a pitch fork and later pitched by hand onto the hay wagon and carried into the barn. The horses were unhitched and driven out of the barn and hitched to a whippletree that was attached to a rope that extended to the top of the barn where a large hay fork (about 20 inches across and 3 feet deep) was hung. Pulling the hay fork to the load of hay, my father would force the fork into the load, as far as possible, by jumping up and down on it. The fork was set by pulling up two prongs. The horses were then driven away from the barn and the rope would pull the hay that was trapped in the fork to the top of the barn, where the fork would catch onto an apparatus that would move the hay over to the hay loft. By pulling a trip rope the hay would fall into a pile.

I was about seven or eight years old when my sister, Pauline, and I had the job of tossing the hay around to the edges of the barn while my father and brother went after another load. The heat under the tin roof would easily hit 120ƒ and, by the time we finished our job, they would be back with another load to be drawn off. When I was eight years old, I acquired the task of driving the team of horses away from the barn to pull the hay to the top of the barn. When the hay got to the place where it could be tripped, my father would yell, "Whoa," and I would stop the horses. Now they had to be backed up the 30 or 40 feet and the whippletree had to be held up in the air so that the horses wouldn't step on it. The whippletree weighed about 30 lbs. I weighed about 60 lbs. I was terrified of that job. I was always frightened that I would get tangled up in the rope and lose a leg or two, or that I might be straddling the rope when it went taut and that I would go flying to the moon or beyond. As I would pull backward with the horses, my sister would pull the slack rope into a small circle ready to draw off the next load. I was always aware that one wrong step would put me in danger of that rope. *I knew very early in life that I was **not** going to be a farmer.*

Spring was plowing and planting. Summer was haying and cultivating. Fall was harvesting, filling the silo and threshing the wheat. Winter was cutting wood for heat and, always, there were the daily chores of milking, gathering eggs, cleaning the eggs, feeding the animals, cleaning the barn, bringing in the wood, churning the butter and, when that was done, there was always something else to do every day, seven days a week.

To think that Samuel Fuller of the Mayflower was a doctor and his son was a preacher and his grandson was also a doctor. I have often wondered which of my grandfathers had sinned and come short of the Glory of God for us to end up in a smelly cow barn or in a hot hay field not looking forward to the next day knowing that it was going to be just like this one if not worse. I knew that I wasn't cut out to spend the rest of my life under a cow trying to squeeze out a few quarts of milk just so that I could run around to the front of her and put some hay and grain into her so that I could start the whole process over again the next morning.

Entertainment

We did have entertainment. The highlight of the week, for most farmers, was to go to town on Saturday night. The stores were all kept open until late at night. Sometimes as late as 8:00 P.M. Keep in mind that there was no daylight saving time until World War II so it was dark shortly after 8:00 P.M. in the summer. The town had a movie theater and adults paid 25 cents, teens paid 10 cents and the under 12 crowd got in *free*. No one cheated on the age deal as everyone knew everyone and birthdays were easily remembered. On many a cold winter night, my two older sisters, Pauline, Beatrice and myself would walk the 2 miles to the village to see a movie. I always got in free, but the walk home on a freezing night was a challenge and I would freeze my tail end on the long walk home. But that was entertainment.

The county fairs were big in the 1930's and 1940's and every county had one. That was the big event to look forward to in the fall. After morning chores the farmers would put on their Sunday best (suit, shirt and tie) and go to the fair for a few hours. They all had to get back home for milking.

My first recollection of the county fair was the Otsego County Fair at Morris, NY around 1937 or 1938. The State Troopers were fairly new as a police force in New York State and they seemed to feel that they had to prove themselves. They started policing with horses and some of the troopers were very fine horsemen led by Police Captain Fox out of Sidney, NY. They would perform some amazing stunts, jumping on and off of horses and doing hand stands etc. While they were performing, there was a large balloon being filled and, at the end of the State Police performance, the balloon went up over the grand stand with some people in the basket under it and everyone was amazed, especially us farm kids. I recall at least one time when a small plane was flying back and forth in front of the grandstand with a crazy man doing all kinds of stunts on the wings. Now that was an eye popper.

We went somewhere to a circus that was in a large tent when I was about 6 years old, and seeing a man shot out of a cannon was the most excitement that I had ever seen or expected to ever see.

Holidays were special. Christmas was super special. My father would go to the woods and cut the top out of a Hemlock tree and we would decorate it with strings of popcorn and paper chains. A painted light bulb hung by a string was additional decoration. Christmas cards were mailed to friends and relatives with a postage stamp costing one and a half cents each, as long as it wasn't sealed. If you sealed it, you were required to pay the full three cents that it cost to mail a letter first class. Dinner with relatives and exchanging small gifts usually costing less than a dime, was exciting. Often a home made toy was a prized gift. Usually two of our biggest roosters gave their lives for our holiday dinners.

The Christmas of 1937 was one to be remembered. We were ready to go to our Grandparents house when our chimney caught fire. We almost always burned green wood as we couldn't get ahead with the wood cutting to allow time for the wood to season. Green wood fills the chimney with creosote and as it dries out it tends to burn and burn it did. The chimney was red hot. My father eventually got it under control and we did have a nice Christmas. My Grandfather had taken a small sheet of plywood and nailed five tin cans onto it and painted it gray. My Grandmother had sewn beans into several little bags and we had a bean bag game that we played with long after my Grandpa died.

In 1940, Montgomery Ward had a single shot BB Gun advertised for $1.98. I knew that I could never have it as it cost so much but I asked Santa for it anyway. Again, it was my Grandparents' turn to have Christmas at their place. One year we would have it, the next year my father's sister, Aunt Bessia Rood, would have it and then the Grandparents. Well, I never was so surprised in my life when after dinner we gathered around the tree and, low and behold, old Santa (In all likelihood with some help) came through. I had my BB Gun. Grandpa died the following August and Christmas was divided between our house and the Rood's.

The Grange

One big highlight would be going to the Grange meetings, which were held once a month on Saturday nights, when many farmers came to town. Actually, the Grange is a fraternal order with its own secret ritual and Edmeston had, and still does have, a Grange Hall. The Grange was formed to help farmers learn advanced farming methods and keep up to date with laws, farm prices and, in general, to learn what was going on in the farming community. However, for most farmers it was a social gathering. The adults would meet upstairs and the farm kids would meet downstairs. All

I can remember about our meetings was our song, "We Are The Grange of the Future," and sneaking sugar cubes from the kitchen. Sometimes we would be invited upstairs when there was a skit being performed or some other type of entertainment was at hand.

Once a year the Dairylea people would bring in all the ice cream that we could eat and I ate all that I could get my hands on. We always looked forward to that event. The fund-raiser was the Grange Bazaar. The entire town was invited and the farm wives would bring cakes, pies and canned goods to be purchased by the poor, unfortunate people that didn't live on farms. We called them the non-farm families. In the summer we had a picnic to look forward to. At Christmas they always had a tree and a small toy for the farm kids. This was often the only toy some of the kids received for Christmas. It was depression time.

To join the Grange one needed to have a sponsor. The sponsor would tell the group what a great asset the prospective member would be. A table would be set up in the middle of the Hall and on it was a large box with a small hole in the top. Next to that box was an additional box of black marbles and white marbles. The Grange pianist would play the Grange Anthem and each member would march around the table and pick up a marble and place it in the large box. After this ritual was completed and everyone was seated, the Grangemaster would open the box. If only one black marble was in the box the new membership was denied. The prospect had been "*Black Balled*."

Edmeston

Let me tell you a little about Edmeston in the 1930's and 1940's. Edmeston, used to support three hardware stores, four grocery stores, a gift shop, two barbers, three feed stores, a farm equipment dealer, two coal dealers, a movie theater, a bowling ally, an ice cream parlor, a drug store, two doctors, a bank, a blacksmith shop, an insurance company, a railroad station for freight, two milk stations, a wood mill, a grist mill, a three-story hotel, a restaurant that competed with both the hotel and ice cream parlor, three garages, a car dealer, and seven businesses with gasoline pumps when gasoline was 16 cents a gallon and a school, "The Otsego School," for children with Down Syndrome. There were two dams, one on each end of town.

Today almost everything is gone. The insurance company has expanded beyond most people's dreams. There is one small grocery (*convenience*) store, one hardware store, one garage and a bank that is no longer the Edmeston Bank. Small town America is almost a thing of past. The small family farms are rapidly disappearing and large corporation farms are taking over; this is one of America's biggest losses.

Edmeston was made up of people from almost every European country. There were Poles, Czechs, Irish, Dutch, English, Germans, Slavs, French, Russians, Jews and Italians. Almost every country was represented. Most were farmers. We didn't always understand each other, but we all got along. They all learned to speak English, albeit the accents were at times a little potent and hard to understand. Even when we didn't understand each other's customs and practices, everyone seemed to accept each other for who they were. They were all hard working and honest families. Many had come to America to find a better life. Many did.

The Green Ring

Fighter for Truth and Justice

It was always a thrill to be able to go to my Grandparents' house for a visit or to Aunt Bessia and Uncle Elbert Rood to spend a night or sometimes a few days. When I was about seven years old the comic books had a hero called, "The Green Hornet." My cousin Stuart had several Green Hornet comic books. I had learned how to read and I was so thrilled by the wonderful things that the Green Hornet could do, that I made up my mind that the world needed another Green Hornet and that would be me.

Since the world already had one Green Hornet, they probably couldn't use two. I would have to have another name but I would do the same marvelous things. I would fly around the country and cities doing good and destroying evil. My dilemma was what to call myself and what kind of kinky outfit should I wear. Both Superman and the Green Hornet were flying around in their long underwear but I didn't like that idea too much. Finally, I solved the puzzle.

My Aunt Bessia had draw shades that pulled down with a draw string that had a green ring on the end to hold on to. This was perfect. I took one of the draw strings with a green ring off of the shade and put it around my neck. Now I was the "Green Ring." Now the world would be safe!

I kept my secret hidden until I returned home. At home I would run and try to take off flying with the green ring around my neck. Nothing happened.

One Sunday, during Sunday School, the teacher gave us a lesson on faith. She said that if we had "The faith as a grain of mustard seed you could move a mountain: and nothing shall be impossible unto you." This was the greatest news that I had ever heard and I just couldn't wait until I could get back home.

I knew what a mustard seed looked like. We sure had plenty of mustard growing wild on the farm. It is a weed with small yellow flowers and are almost impossible to get rid of. I picked some mustard when we got home and looked at the little seeds and I knew that I certainly could conjure up faith larger than that little mustard seed. I put several mustard seeds into my pocket and I ran to the house and got my hidden Green Ring. I put it around my neck and took off running expecting to take off at any time flying like I was supposed to.

Nothing happened.

I remember the preacher saying that "Prayer changes things." Maybe that was the issue. I hadn't prayed. So I prayed. Tried the running bit again and still nothing happened. Well, maybe I needed a "*take off*" place. Maybe sometimes God needs a little help.

Behind the house was a hill and I ascended to the top. Now, I was really going to test my faith. I backed off a little from the top of the hill and I prayed, just like I was supposed to, and a little harder than usual. I made every kind of promise as to how I would rid the world of evil, and how I was going to give God a helping hand that I was most assured that he needed. I said, "Lord, to make it easier on You, I will take a flying leap off the top of this hill so that you won't have such a hard time getting me off of the ground and together we will do great and wonderful things."

Well, I took off on the fastest run that I had ever run. I took a flying leap into the air and WOW!!! .... I was actually flying. What a wonderful thrill. Just like the Green Hornet and just like Superman. You can't even imagine the excitement for a seven year old boy to actually be flying through the air. I knew that the world would be different from now on.

But ..... something terrible happened.

Somehow the ground got in the way. It literally came up to meet me and at a rather fast pace too. I hit with a wallop and went tail over teakettle. I stopped somewhere in the middle of the hill, cut and bruised but no broken bones. This was appalling. My self-esteem and my faith completely collapsed. I took those mustard seeds and tossed them as far as I could and went crying to the house. I never picked up any more mustard seeds or green rings.

Tony and Queenie

The team of horses that we had in the mid-30's, were a couple of aging mares. My father felt that it was time to raise a couple of colts for their replacement. They were both bred and one had a male that we named Tony, the other had a female that we named Queenie. It was great fun watching the little ones follow their mothers as they pulled the wagon or sleigh or any other piece of farm equipment. They would run along next to the adults and in this way they learned what "whoa" and "get up," or the sucking noise made in the mouth for a signal to "get going" all meant. Later, a harness would be put on the young colts and they would be taught how to respond to all of the various commands, etc. Finally, when Tony and Queenie were about 2 years old, and much bigger than their mothers, they were ready to do the job that they were raised for. The mothers were sold at auction and my father put the high spirited team to work.

They had learned to stand in the barn, hitched to the manure wagon, while my father and my older brother, Bob, would clean the barn. They had learned how to move ahead a little way, when commanded to, until the entire barn was cleaned.

One day, after the manure was loaded onto the wagon, my father ushered the team and the wagon out of the barn. He stopped the team and went back to close the barn door. We had a small puppy that loved to nip at the horses ankles and he perceived this as his opportunity. Before my father could return to the wagon, Tony and Queenie were off and running down the road that led into the village, with the wagon bouncing and the manure flying and my frantic father in hot pursuit.

We didn't see my father, Tony or Queenie or the manure wagon for about an hour or so, when up the road came Tony and Queenie pulling the wagon with my father in it. It seems that when the horses raced through the village, no one could stop them, until they had made their way all the way to the milk station at the other end of the village. There some men did get them halted. They had run over three miles with a wagon full of manure. It wasn't so full coming home, so the trip back was easier for the horses. My guess is that it wasn't so easy for my humbled father. He looked awfully sheepish coming up the road with only a small part of his original load. I guess that the village was well fertilized that morning. That didn't seem to help the village any, as it never seemed to grow. My father was embarrassed almost to tears. I asked my mother what was the matter with Dad. She said that "He had egg on his face." *It didn't look like egg to me.*

Getting Rid Of Old Fred

In the 1930's and in the early 1940's, there wasn't any social security for the old folks. Most either lived with relatives or had to depend on charity, if they had no money. Some were just to proud too accept charity and tried to keep on working. Old Fred Burlison was one of these people. The problem was that he was rather feeble and couldn't really do much work, and he was a cantankerous old goat on top of that. So the farmers had come to some kind of an agreement that they would share the old guy and *pretend* that he was their hired man. Our turn came in January of 1941. It seemed like a good deal, as my brother had turned 18 and had left home to seek his fortune in Florida. We could use another hand, as I had just turned nine years old and I was rather small. We were scared to death of old Fred. He hated kids and we kind of didn't like Old Fred either. We actually feared coming home from school and weekends were a disaster. Old Fred seemed to think that he had taken over the place and, in a way, he had. Everyone had to jump at his demands and he didn't think that we had enough chores to do. He could always think of some new ones for us and we did them. No one argued with Old Fred. Even my father didn't argue with Old Fred. Even Old Fred didn't argue with Old Fred.

We didn't have a place for old Fred to sleep in this small farm house. Almost every farm house had what we called, a parlor. This was a special room where only the real good furniture was kept. It was used only on special occasions, such as when we had company in the summer and on Christmas day in the winter. We had a stove in our parlor. It was only used on Christmas day or on a Sunday afternoon, if we had company, which was extremely rare. It was decided to put Old Fred in the parlor. Old Fred now had the best room in the house and, on top of that, he was allowed to use the stove for heat.

The rooms upstairs had no heat, except for the chimney pipe from the wood burning furnace that we had in the cellar. Since the furnace pipe ran up through the living room and into an attic over the living room, my brother and I would sleep on a mattress in the attic in the winter. Four of my sisters slept in the room over the parlor. With Old Fred in the parlor and with the stove burning they had heat from the stove pipe. My brother was gone, so I slept in my own room next to my four older sisters with the door open so as to enjoy some of the little heat that escaped from the chimney.

Since the toilet was out doors we were allowed a chamber pot to be kept under our bed with a lid on it to use in the night. It was to be emptied every morning. I didn't always "*remember*" to empty my chamber pot and, in fact, it had somehow become rather full, so one night I sneaked out into the girls' bedroom to use their pot. As it turned out the girls hadn't emptied their pot either. It too was full but I didn't notice that until I had the pot out from underneath the bed and bent down to use it. As I kneeled down to use it, my knee hit the edge of the pot and the pot tipped over onto the floor and: "*Water water* [*slop*] *everywhere.*" Now where was all of this "*used*" water to go? Where else but right for the hot stove pipe and on down the pipe to the stove below. Now a hot stove pipe has a way of sizzling and steaming when water of any kind hits it and when this kind of liquid hits it, it has a tendency to steam and stink. I mean really stink. Well, of course, it woke up Old Fred. The entire parlor was a stinking, steaming mess and poor Old Fred just completely lost his cool and let out every profanity that he could marshal and in the process he woke everyone up everyone in the house. My little secret was no longer a secret. Now I had Old Fred screaming at me along with four older sisters but my mother started to laugh and my father was kept busy trying to settle Old Fred down.

I don't remember where they put Old Fred for the night as he couldn't sleep in the parlor but I remember dreading to come home from school the next afternoon because I was sure that I would have to face the wrath of old Fred. But when we got home, Old Fred was gone. I never saw Old Fred again. We never asked any questions but we used to joke that maybe our father had called the S.P.C.A. (Society for the Prevention of Cruelty to Animals) and had Old Fred put out of his misery. We heard rumors that our father had trucked Old Fred to the next farm so that they could take advantage of having a "*hired man*" a little earlier than they might have expected. I think that the rumors were true as I can remember the neighbors not speaking to any of us for an extended period of time.

The Hinman Milker

In the summer of 1941 my older brother, Bob, was in the U.S. Army. He had joined shortly after returning from Florida in March. Old Fred was gone and our little sister, Barbara, was too small to help out on the farm. My oldest sister, Vesta, was married and gone. Dorotha and Beatrice had jobs in the village so they were gone. Pauline was 12 and I was 9 and we did our best but it was hard on our father to keep up with all of the work. Bob had always been an exceptional worker and a good farmer and we missed him.

Pauline and I could only milk a total of a couple of cows in the morning and 4 or 5 in the evening as we had other chores to do too. Our Uncle Elbert had a milking machine that he could run directly off his Delco generator. Our father thought maybe he could do the same thing but money was scarce.

A Hinman Milking Machine salesman came to the farm and he had a *"fantastic"* deal on a used Hinman milking machine. He offered to demonstrate it. The machine was set up and the vacuum pipes were only put in place for the first two cows as this was only a demonstration. My father fired up the generator and the salesman went to place the teat cup on the cows teat and it became apparent that there was an electrical short somewhere. Now the generator only generated enough electricity to charge the batteries to 32 volts but apparently when used directly it had a little more zap. When the salesman touched the cow we heard a loud **"Blaaat"** and the cow was on her knees and she suddenly jumped through her stanchion. That was the end of the Hinman Milker and the salesman. There was a rumor that someone wrote a short poem about the cow and the Hinman Milker. It was something about some cat and a fiddle and something about a cow jumping over the moon.

Birthing

We were not allowed any kind of sex education. Sex was a four letter word and was not to be used. The penalty was death or worse. Living on a farm with all kinds of farm animals, reproduction was an every day kind of thing but we weren't supposed to know anything about it. We were kept exceptionally ignorant in that area. Every time something exciting was about to happen, my father would send us kids to the house. For years I thought that my middle name was "*Go To The House.*" If you had asked me my name I would have told you that it was Ray Go To The House Fuller.

One Sunday morning, we had a brood sow that delivered a record number of piglets. I don't remember the exact number but I recall that she had more piglets than she had dinner places. Our father was so proud that he even went to church albeit only to brag about his brood sow. He invited the Rood's up for dinner. While my mother and my Aunt Bessia were preparing dinner, the rest of us went down to the barn to look at the pigs. While we were admiring the litter, the sow had another piglet. I was never so excited in my life. Neither was my father. All I heard was "Ray Go To The House" and I did. I ran as fast as I could, bursting with excitement, and I told my Aunt Bessia and my mother that the sow had another pig and "do you want to know where it came from?" Before they could answer my question, I told them where the little fellow came from because I was certain that they too would want to know. Well, they must have been as shocked as I was because they changed my name to "Ray Stay In The House."

We always had young calves on the farm and they would run around and play much like children. One day when I went to the barn to do my chores, there was a cow that seemed to be in a great deal of pain and my father was pulling on two hind legs that were sticking out of the back of the cow. The cow was making all kinds of painful noises. It was obvious that she was in a great deal of distress. My father noticed my presence and immediately started calling out my name, "Ray Go To The House." I knew that the legs looked like the legs of a calf but how he got in there was a mystery to me. I hid behind some other cows to watch the action. The cow broke from her stanchion and my father hung on to those little legs for dear life. The cow ran from one end of the barn to the other and my father was almost flying through the air but he still hung on. I had no idea as to what was happening. I didn't know what birthing was much less a breach birth. Finally the calf dropped.

My father was leaning up against another cow all bent over and gasping for breath and sweating in great profusion. I walked out from my hiding place and said, "Gee Dad, how did he get in there?" Between gasps for his breath, he feebly declared, "I don't know!". I said, "I'll bet that he will watch were he's going the next time, won't he, Dad?" As unsteady, shaky and worn-out as my Dad was, he could still assemble a vigorous. "Go To The House."

School

Your Grandpa Ray turned 5 years old on January 1, 1937. In September, I started school in the first grade. My sister, Beatrice, took me to my room to meet my teacher, Mrs. Ackerman. First grade was learning basics. We did learn our ABC's and some reading and some writing with pencils as big as my arm and taking naps after lunch on our little rugs that were kept in the closet.

Farm Rats

At the end of my first school year, I was awakened in the morning by rats chewing on my toes. On the farm we were forever fighting the rat problem in the barn and often they found that the house was a good place for food and shelter. No one would believe me when I came down stairs crying that rats had chewed my toes until they looked at the bloody mess. My mother soaked my foot in Epson Salts and wrapped it with some kind of black (coal tar) ointment and sent me off to school as it was the last day of the school year. With soaking and wrapping in ointment my toes healed without any serious problems. We didn't have the dollar for an office call at Doc Granger's so we healed ourselves as best we could.

Depression Time Shoes and My Little Red Boots

In the 1930's there were times that we went barefoot in the summer but not because we wanted to. Our shoes were worn out and, unless someone gave us some used shoes, there wouldn't be any new ones until fall when we would go to Schworms Store and for $2.00 each we got new shoes. They weren't very good shoes. The soles would soon come loose, especially if they got wet, and they would flop, flop, flop as we walked down the school halls. Since all of the farm women did a great deal of canning, we all had a big supply of used red jar rubbers that we would place around the toe and middle of the shoes to stop the flopping. The jar rubbers would wear out rather quickly so many of us carried a pocket full of used jar rubbers for immediate emergency repairs.

No usable used clothing was discarded in the 1930's or the 1940's. Someone could always use outgrown clothing. There wasn't any problem with "*out-dated*" clothing. Clothing was clothing. Styles meant nothing in farm country.

One day someone had given us a box of used clothing and in it was a pair of little red rubber boots that fit me. I cherished those little red boots and I proudly wore them around the farm. There was a place in front of the old barn that actually became a sinkhole when the earth got wet. We called it the quick sand hole and we were frightened of it, especially in the spring. One evening while our father was in the barn milking, my sister, Pauline, taunted me into stepping into the sinkhole with (as she called them) my "*fancy*" red boots. I stepped into the mire and suddenly found myself sinking rather fast. The more I struggled the faster I was sinking and both of us soon were screaming for help. Our father came out of the barn demanding to know what all of the uproar was about. He soon realized that it wasn't going to be very long and his future farm hand would be out of sight, so he grabbed me and pulled me out. The suction of the sink hole kept my little red boots and I cried and cried for those red boots.

After the old barn burned down and the new barn was built, the sink hole was covered over by the newly built milk house. Today an addition to the barn has been added and it now covers that old sinkhole and my precious little red boots.

Reading and Writing

My second grade teacher, Mrs. George, taught us to read and write. Your parents will tell you that I never forgot the first poem that I had to learn in the second grade and I have bored them more than once with it. I am going to bore you with it here. The book was illustrated and the poem went like this:

If all the men were one man
what a great man that would be.   *Now if the great man*
If all the axes were one ax   *took the great ax*
what a great ax that would be.   *and cut down the great tree*
If all the trees were one tree   *and let it fall into the great sea*
what a great tree that would be.   *what a splish-splash*
If all the seas were one sea   *that would be.*
what a great sea that would be.

My First True Love

During my second grade a new girl came to our school. Her name was Ruth Morford and I was in love. One never forgets his first love. This was the real thing. Every morning when Ruth Morford came into the room I would affectionately kiss Ruth Morford on her sweet and adorable cheek.

Ruth Morford didn't finish out the school year. She moved away and I never saw her again. When I told my older sister, Pauline, how much my heart was broken and, how often, and how lovingly I had kissed Ruth Morford every morning, my sister insisted that I had gotten Ruth Morford in the family way and in order to save face she had to leave town. I didn't kiss any girls for a long, long time after Ruth Morford.

New School House—New Kids

I started third grade in the fall of 1939 at the age of seven in a brand new school building with Mrs. Larson as my teacher.

During the depression, President Roosevelt tried many things to help pull the country out of the turmoil that the entire nation was suffering. One thing that he did was to offer low cost loans and federal grants to build highways, bridges and schools. Edmeston, received a *WPA Grant in

1938 and centralized and immediately started building a large brick school building. The building was completed in 1939. They eventually closed all of the little one room school houses in the district and bused the kids to Edmeston. This included the towns of West Burlington, Burlington Flats, Burlington Green, Exeter, North Edmeston and all of the little satellites scattered throughout the district. This gave us a much larger class of about 20 kids.

*WPA was a federal government agency called Works Progress Administration until 1939 when the name was changed to Works Projects Administration. The WPA was terminated during the war in 1943.

The Barn Fire

One night in October of 1939, my father had been on the second floor of the barn husking corn until late in the evening. A thunder storm came up and he went to the house and was washing up and getting ready to go to bed when he saw a bright flash of lightning and heard a loud crash of thunder. He looked out the window and saw that the barn was on fire. The barn had been hit by lightning and it burned to the ground.

It was a warm October night and the cows had been let out to pasture for the night so they were safe. My father managed to get most of the live stock out, including the horses, out of the barn but the barn was gone along with the hay and all of the farm tools that were in an attached shed. Also missing were about 20 farm cats. Cats were always allowed to roam the farms to keep the mouse population down and they pretty much made their living on their own. We did keep a pan out in the milk house and every time we strained the milk we would remove the foam from the strainer and place it in the pan for the cats. The Delco generator was in the barn and it too was lost so we didn't have any kind of lights for the house. Farmers carried little or no insurance during the depression. Things were very desperate.

A man named Norwood Robinson lived about two miles on the East side of the village and he had an empty barn. He called my father and a deal was made to use his barn but it was four miles away and we had 30 cows that had to be moved that day. My father and my brother, Robert, drove the cattle down the dirt road to the village, on down North Street, made a left turn up East Street and on toward West Burlington for two more miles. The cows had a home. Hay and feed were bought on credit and the milk house was repaired to pass inspection. Everything fell into place rather rapidly but with one major problem. How to milk cows that are four miles away.

The solution was to rent an apartment in the village of Edmeston. We moved to town. Wow!! We had real electricity. We had real running water. We had an indoor toilet. We had kids to play with. We were really living the good life and my mother was the happiest that she had been in years. Oh how she loved living in the village. People to visit with, things to do, places to go. This was where the action was and we all loved it.

My sister, Beatrice, came down with Scarlet Fever. A yellow and black sign was posted on the front of our residence and everyone was quarantined out of the house for at least 6 weeks. My sister, Pauline, and I stayed at our Grandparents' during that time. Bob and my father procured some army cots and slept in the barn with the cows. My sister, Barbara, had to stay home. No one could enter or leave until the quarantine was lifted.

In the spring of 1940 both my father and brother started to work on building a new barn. Trees were cut for lumber from our woods and lumber was also purchased on credit. By late summer we had a new barn. As much as everyone hated it, we were back on the farm. The new Delco generator was placed in the cellar of the house. The cows were in the new barn and I was eight years old and in the fourth grade. My brother, Bob, was getting itchy feet. He wanted to see some country besides Edmeston. He and another farm boy had gone to the New York Worlds Fair in New York City for a few days in 1939 and he knew that a bigger world was out there. After the harvest in the fall he took his Model A Ford and packed all of his belongings in it and headed for Miami, Florida. He spent the winter in Miami, milking cows on a huge dairy farm. He returned in March of 1941, helped out on the farm for a few days and then joined the army.

My Father's World Closes In On Him

1941 was an extremely hard year. I was nine years old and the family was beginning to break up. My brother and the three oldest sisters had left home. Bob was in the army, Vesta was married, Beatrice and Dorotha had jobs.

That left only my sister, Pauline, and myself to help out on the farm. Barbara was only 6 years old so she couldn't do any work. The final blow was my mother needed major surgery and, she ended up in the hospital for several weeks. Even though in the fall of 1940 my father had sponsored a couple of barn dances in the new barn to help pay for the building, he was still heavily in debt. He was all alone with a big farm to run and only 2 kids to help and we were very young and small. To top it all off, we hated being back on the farm and he knew it. Oh, how we hated it, especially our mother. She had had a taste of village life and she longed for the village as did I.

My father was what you might call a binge drinker. He would not drink anything for several weeks or even several months but when he started drinking he would often disappear for several days. It seems that drinking was his only release and in the fall of 1940 he was really depressed and drinking heavily. He was starting to realize that he was going to have to run this farm almost by himself. We all hated the farm and no one had wanted to come back to it. My mother was not happy. The older children had left home or were leaving. He started drinking very heavily after we returned to the farm. He was completely drunk for both of the barn dances. He just got worse. In the early spring of 1941 after my mother ended up in the hospital and with almost everyone gone, he really took to the bottle.

Beatrice came home to run the house while my mother was in the hospital. Pauline and I had our chores to do. Beatrice was supposed to get us both up at 6:00 A.M. to go to the barn and do our chores. My mother used to sit down at her piano and start playing some of her favorite songs at about 6:00 o'clock in the morning to wake us kids up. She would play and sing until we came downstairs, dressed and ready to go to the barn. Now she was in the hospital.

One morning Pauline had gotten up but I overslept. Beatrice was busy fixing breakfast and didn't realize that I was still in bed. At about 6:30 my father came to the house in a rage. He dragged me out of my nice warm bed and, before I could even finish dressing, he headed me for the barn and for every step that I took I got a work boot on my backside from him. I was supposed to be up in the silo pitching down the ensilage. He had already sent Pauline up and she was tossing the ensilage down the shoot. He wouldn't let her stop throwing down the ensilage while I climbed up the silo ladder. I was covered with ensilage. It was in my hair and in my clothing. Pauline climbed down the ladder and went to the hay loft to pitch down the hay and I finished pitching down the ensilage and later finished my other chores including milking one cow. Now it was time for school.

Now let me give you an idea how ensilage smells. One of the local farmers received an invitation from the Internal Revenue Service to go to Syracuse, NY for a tax audit. The night before his scheduled trip he went into his silo and buried a pair of coveralls in the ensilage. The next morning he took the coveralls and wrapped them up in a burlap bag and put them in the trunk of his car and drove to Syracuse. He parked his car in a parking lot, took out the coveralls and put them on, gathered up his papers and headed for the IRS office. When he entered the office he received immediate attention. People in the waiting room found a reason to step aside and some even left the room. He announced to the receptionist that he was there for his audit and she immediately, ushered him into a cubicle and introduced him to the auditor. The auditor took a quick gaze at the papers presented to him and holding his breath he suddenly announced that perhaps there had been a mistake and told the farmer that his records were in perfect order and dismissed him immediately. [Keep this in mind if you are ever called in for a tax audit.]

My case was a little different. Remember, we didn't have a bath tub or a shower on the farm so I went to school with ensilage in my hair and in my clothes The teacher left the room and in a very short time she returned and said to me that a boy in the first grade really needed a shower and would I help her out by taking him to the school shower. This is called diplomacy. After the other boy and I had showered there were some nice clean clothes waiting for me. Where they came from I have no idea but as I started to get dressed the teacher noticed the bruises all over my backside. My cousin, Irene Rood, had finished her nurses training in Utica and was now the school nurse and I was taken to her. I told her what had happened and she took me to stay with her family for awhile. I thought, wow, a vacation at the Rood's and during the school year too. What a treat. I didn't realize that I was being removed from my home.

After a few days my Aunt Bessia and cousin, Irene, drove me back to the farm and advised me that my father wanted to speak to me. I went to the barn where he was milking cows and he started crying. I had never seen my father cry before. He said to me that if I would come home that he would never hit me again. I didn't know that I had a choice. He tried to tell me that he loved me in his own way by telling me that someday this whole farm would be mine. I ran from the barn crying and went back to my aunt and cousin to tell them that "Dad wants me to take over the farm...he wants to give it to me and I hate it here," It took the two of them and my sister, Pauline, to convince me that he didn't mean "*today*." He meant that he was going to leave it to me someday but the danger of that ever happening was from slim to none, and they sent me back to the barn.

I don't remember my father ever apologizing to me before that incident for anything. He commenced crying again. Again, he asked me to forgive him. Again, he promised "never to strike me again."

I agreed to come home and...

He kept his promise.

TWO

Growing Up

By 1938 my older siblings were grown and ready to leave the nest. My oldest sister, Vesta, was married on June 25, 1938. Dorotha was working part time at the *Otsego School for Backward Children and was living there much of the time. By the end of 1940, Bob had left home and Beatrice had a job, baby sitting for the Baptist minister and his wife and was staying with them in the village.

Note: The Otsego School was a school owned and operated by a Miss Florence Chesebrough, a registered nurse and it was for the well to do people that could afford semi-private care for children with Down Syndrome. We called them Mongoloid children. Today these children might be called children with learning disabilities. The school (named, The Otsego School for Backward Children) is no longer in existence. The State of New York bought out the heirs and built a new and beautiful village on the outskirts of Edmeston, called The Pathfinder Village, open to almost everyone that has a need. Miss Chesebrough adopted two boys and raised them. A single woman adopting two boys in the 1930's was almost unheard of. I grew up with these two boys, David and John. We were good friends all through school. John married a local girl, Anna Claire Lockerbie, and they raised their family in Edmeston. Dave went on to college and became, first a Baptist minister, later a college professor.

I Learn To Milk Cows

Early in 1940, when Old Fred came up missing and the older kids were gone, only Pauline and I were big enough to help out on the farm. One day our father came home with a present for my sister, Pauline, and one for me. We weren't accustomed to receiving gifts of any kind, especially if it wasn't Christmas or our birthday and we were very excited until we saw what it was.

Some wonderful person had invented a new kind of milking stool. I had just turned nine and my sister, Pauline, wasn't yet twelve and we were not big enough to hold a milk pail between our legs to milk a cow. However, this remarkable invention had an extension to the milk stool so that you could set a pail on it. Now even little kids could milk cows. What a great idea. We learned to milk cows in two easy lessons. We now had to milk a cow every morning and two every evening on top of doing our other chores. We had to pitch down the hay and ensilage and feed the cows. All at once, Old Fred seemed intensely acceptable. We realized that he did do some work on the farm but now he was gone. It's like they say, "You don't miss the water until the well runs dry." We wanted Old Fred even if he was half dead.

Farm Cats

Our cat population had again increased very rapidly and by now we were back up to the two dozen or so cats. These were not your typical lap cat. They were undomesticated. You couldn't approach one to pet it but they would come around at milking time prepared to lick up the froth taken from the milk strainer. Every now and then one would get brave and walk down the middle of the barn behind the cows. Pauline and I found it great sport to shoot at these brave little critters with a stream of milk directly from the cows teat. We would giggle every time we made a direct hit and the poor little animal would run as if the sky was falling. We had one cat that figured out very quickly that the white stream coming his way was real milk and he liked real milk. We learned that by squirting the stream of milk just ahead of him that he would chase it. We almost fell off our stools laughing. We would then redirect the stream of milk behind him and he would do a back flip chasing it. It took our father only a short time to figure out what we found to be so entertaining about milking cows and he put a stop to that in a hurry, or so he thought. Every so often, when he was taking his milk pail to the milk house and we were left in the barn alone, some unsuspecting cat would get a little surprise and we would get to giggle just a little more. We learned to embrace our small pleasures whenever one became available.

Raining Goats

In 1941, Pauline and I got it into our heads that we wanted to have a goat. Since we all disliked the farm so much our father did all he could to make us happy and he gave in and let us both have a baby (kid) goat. The problem with little goats is that they grow into big goats. Big goats often develop a personality of their own, with an unfavorable disposition, and can become difficult to handle. One evening in the early spring of 1942, after we had finished our milking and other chores, we took our goats out of their pens to exercise them. Somehow they both got away from us and Pauline went chasing after them. When the new barn was built, the milk house was built in front of the barn, it backed up to a bank so that the back of the milk house roof was almost even with the ground and the front of the milk house would have about a 7 foot drop. As Pauline was chasing the goats they decided their best escape route was the milk house roof. When they observed that they were cornered with no where to go, they both jumped off of the roof just at the same time our father was coming out of the barn to the milk house with a pail of milk in each hand. I think that he thought that the sky was falling, but it really was only a couple of goats. With the shock of goats falling from the sky directly in front of him to the point of almost hitting him, our father dropped both pails of milk. Pauline got the scolding of her life. Our father thought that she had done this to be entertaining and I thought that it was about the funniest thing that I had ever seen. Somehow those goats disappeared the next day. Someone got my goat. It wasn't amusing anymore.

Sheep Farming in Edmeston

In the late 1930's my sister, Beatrice, joined the 4H Club. This club was designed to direct the energies of the young farm kids in the right direction. The girls mostly learned how to cook, bake, sew and embroider. They also, like the boys, were required to have a project such as raising a farm animal. Somehow the 4H leader thought that Edmeston would be a magnificent place to raise sheep. Suddenly sheep started making their appearance on farms all over the county. Beatrice acquired two lambs and raised them for several months but in Edmeston there really wasn't any place to market the wool and almost no demand for their meat. We arrived home one afternoon from school and found a couple of sheep skins on the second floor of the barn. They had been butchered. We tried to eat the meat but no one favored mutton, and besides, these guys had been our little buddies.

Our cousin, Stuart Rood, also had joined the 4H and he enjoyed raising sheep very much. His father allowed him to section off an ample segment of hill land and he started his little sheep ranch. Before long he became educated to the fact that sheep were not a good commodity for the town of

Edmeston. He had worked his project for about three years before he finally gave up on them. We were never certain how many sheep he had accumulated over the short interval that he was the *good shepherd* because every time we tried to count them we fell asleep.

"Doc" Pine

A little old man lived in the village on East Street that everyone referred to as Doctor Pine or more frequently as "Doc Pine." He wasn't a licensed medical doctor. He was an Indian (Native American) and it was said that he was the 7th son of a 7th son. It was also rumored that he was born with a skin veil over his face and all of these things were supposed to give him a special power. I don't know how much of all of that was true, or if it was strictly legend, but I know that he did have some kind of special powers. This man was a great believer in herbal cures and often ventured into the Adirondack Mountains to find rare herbs. His house was much like a herbal drug store.

I could write about several people that claimed to have been miraculously cured of different ailments by this man but these accounts would all be hearsay. Let me tell you what I really know.

One evening when my sister, Barbara, was about six or seven years old, Pauline was giving her a piggy back ride upstairs in the new barn. We had a hole cut in the floor on both sides of the barn to pitch hay down to the cow mangers below. Somehow Barbara fell off and toppled down the hole and landed on the concrete floor below. Although she was knocked unconscious, her injuries didn't look at all serious. A few days later she began to have a slight tremor in her hands. It got progressively worse and in a short time she had the shakes all over. She was taken to Dr. Granger and he acknowledged that this problem was not something that he could work with so he referred her to doctors at the Cooperstown Hospital. After Xrays and doing several tests, they advised our parents that there was nothing that could be done for her. She had suffered some severe nerve injuries that couldn't be operated on or healed. They said that the problem would only get progressively worse, until finally she wouldn't have any control of any kind, and the prognosis was fatal. Other doctors were consulted and all agreed. It was only to be a matter of time.

I had never seen my parents so somber and so frantic. One day, Barbara was shaking and trembling all over and was in a very critical physical state. My mother suggested that they take her to see Dr. Pine. I had never heard of Dr. Pine before. My father said that he didn't believe in Dr. Pine and was reluctant to go to see the "quack." I recall my mother agreeing with him regarding his being a "quack" but she was determined to try something, anything. They agreed and left for the village with Barbara. It wasn't more than an hour or two when they returned. Barbara was no longer shaking and trembling.

My mother told us that when they walked into his office, Dr. Pine said to Barbara, "You have taken a pretty good fall, haven't you?" He sat her down on a chair next to him and started to work his fingers up and down her spine. He explained that she had some nerves that were damaged and, out of place. In a few minutes she stopped trembling and she walked out of that place completely cured.

Dr. Pine could not charge for his services. He lived on whatever donations people left in the box on the table in the front room of the house that he used for a waiting room. I don't know how much they paid Dr. Pine but, they often agreed that it could never be enough.

Shortly after this episode, my eyes started blinking. I mean really blinking. I couldn't watch a movie as I blinked so much and so often. The kids at school started calling me blinky. One Saturday night the family was going to be treated to a movie in the village. My father said that there was no use in my going as I wouldn't see any of it anyhow. My mother said, " Let's go see Dr. Pine." We did. Doc Pine sat me on a chair next to him. He started rubbing the back of my neck, he came up behind my ears and across the side of my face working his fingers all of the time. We hadn't told him that we were going to the movies but he simply said to me, "Go and enjoy the movie." I did. I have never had an abnormal blinking problem since that night.

In the ninth grade I attempted to catch a football. The ball hit my thumb and knocked it out of joint. The coach gave it one big yank and advised me that he had put the joint back in place. After school, when I went to peddle my papers, my thumb was twice the size that it used to be and it was throbbing. I was riding my bike back down East Street and I hurt so bad that I couldn't stand it. I stopped in at Dr. Pine's office. He looked at me and said, "You aren't supposed to catch a football with your thumb." He sat me down and took my hand and started to gently rub my wrist and kept gently working along to the joint. That joint slid into place so easy that I never felt it. Immediately the pain was gone but the swelling remained. He said to go home and have my mother go out to the garden and take the outside leaves of a cabbage head and put them in the oven until they start to smell real bad and to wrap them around my thumb and wrist. She thought that that was the craziest thing to do but she had become a believer in Dr. Pine, so I soon had smelly cabbage wrapped around my wrist and it did work. The swelling soon subsided.

My Grandfather

Thomas Leander Fuller

1862-1940

My grandfather, Thomas Leander Fuller, and my grandmother, Vesta Fuller lived on a small farm about 3 miles south of the village of Edmeston. My grandma had a car. It was a Ford Model T. It was never driven in the winter.

It had to be cranked to get it started and it was shifted by the use of foot pedals. My sister, Pauline, and I used to get to stay with our grandparents sometimes and the ride to the village was about all the excitement that we ever got at our grandma's. When our grandpa went to town he drove his horse and surrey. He only had one horse.

To do his plowing he would use a one bottom plow that he would hitch to the horse and he followed along behind to guide it. That is a very difficult task. His cultivator was also horse drawn and I found out by experience that holding the cultivator upright and keeping it between the rows of corn was a real challenge. They had a barn with 2 or 3 milk cows for their own use. They made their own butter and cheese and their only cash crop was from egg laying hens. They were poor people. My grandpa almost never spoke. He didn't hear very well so he seldom entered into conversations. He was a very quiet man and walked kind of bent over. He was a kind and gentle sort of person but I do remember his giving me a chewing out once. It was the spring of 1940 when I was sent down to his farm to help him plant his corn. He didn't have a corn planter so he planted it by hand. He had the ground ready and I was to drop 5 kernels to each hill at a certain distance and he would cover them with his hoe. Being only 8 years old at the time it didn't make a vast difference to me if I put 5 or 50 seeds to the hill but it did to my grandpa. Seed corn was costly and there was a depression. Grandpa became very angry with me and he appropriately scolded me. I felt bad that my grandpa had admonished me. He became seriously ill that summer and died on August 21st. Our grandmother had to sell the farm and go do housekeeping for other people as there was no social security or anything else for old people to live on. She died on April 20, 1955 at her daughter's home, my Aunt Bessia Rood. She died just like my father died, sitting in her chair. She was resting after helping to clean her rooms

My Grandpa's Bull

In the 1930's it was unusual for a farmer not to have a bull. Everyone had a bull. Even my grandpa had a bull and he only had 2 or 3 cows. There was a larger farm diagonally across the road from my grandpa's. They had over 30 cows and only one bull. The pastures were next to each other with just a barbed wire fence separating them. The bulls usually roamed the pastures with the cows unless the bull was too treacherous or untrustworthy to be let out.

My sister, Pauline, and I were spending a few days with our grandparents during our summer vacation. It came time for milking. She was ten years old and I was seven. We were old enough to go get our grandpa's cows from the pasture. Both bulls were in their pastures with their harem. Our grandpa's barn was across the road from the house and behind the barn was a small creek and a small hill. We walked up the hill and as we broke over the top of the knoll, we were about 50

yards (about 1/2 the length of a football field) from the cows and
grandpa's bull. Grandpa's bull was not in good humor. We
had only made a few steps toward the cows when we noticed
that the bull was looking over the fence at the neighbor's
cows and he was pawing the ground and snorting rather
loudly. We noticed that, on the other side of the fence, one
of the neighbors cows was in a very romantic mood and the
neighbor's bull was taking full advantage of the situation.
Grandpa's bull was glassy eyed with envy. Pauline and I were
mesmerized. We just stood there watching when suddenly
grandpa's bull seemed to take notice of us. He turned and
started to race toward us. We initiated a rather accelerated
course in the direction of the barn. We had a 50 yard head
start but mad bulls can run very fast. So can two terrified
kids but they are no match for an angry and love deprived
bull. My mind was racing as fast as I was. I knew that my
demise was inescapable. I could already see the epitaph on
my tombstone:

> *Here's what's left of Grandpa Ray*
> *He didn't make it through the day.*
> *His grandpa sent him to do a job*
> *But he ended up a messy blob.*

I thought about mortality and the possibility that I was soon
to experience it...*and the bull kept coming on*. I thought that I was
going to perish and that I would never see home again...*and
the bull kept coming on*. Here is a Baptist boy praying "Hail Mary

Full of Grace, Pray for Us Runners, Now and In This Hour of Our Death!!!"...*and the bull kept coming on*. "Our Father Which Art In Heaven, Give Us This Day Our Fastest Legs."...*and the bull kept coming on*. I prayed for the Green Hornet, Superman or even the Green Ring but no Green Hornet, no Superman and certainly no Green Ring ever showed up...*and the bull kept coming on*. I knew that praying to become the Green ring was probably kind of absurd but I prayed for the Green Ring phenomenon anyhow...*and the bull kept coming on*. I thought about mustard seed and faith, hope and charity...*and the bull kept coming on*. I promised to be more agreeable to my little sister, Barbara, and to cherish her both now and forever more, Amen...*and the bull kept coming on*. I prayed that if You can't help me, just maybe, You could kind of slow down that bull...*and the bull kept coming on*. I made a promise that I would be a much better person...a much, much, much better person, perhaps the pride of the family, the cream of the crop. I would be the best person that He ever knew or that He could ever hope to know...*and the bull kept coming on*. I prayed that maybe He could help me to keep just one step ahead of my sister, Pauline...two would be better but one would give me a little margin...*and the bull kept coming* on. Pauline must have been praying the same prayer and getting her prayer answered, as she was about two steps ahead of me...*and the bull kept coming on*. The barn door was open. We jumped the creek. We made it into the barn...*and the bull kept coming on*. We closed the barn door .... *and the bull kept coming on*. We heard a resounding thud on the door. Pieces of wood came flying off the door and into the barn... *The bull was no longer coming on.*

When we told our grandpa what had happened, he abruptly departed to salvage his cows. We were concerned as our grandpa was rather feeble, but he assured us that he knew what to do and that he could deal with his own bull. The bull didn't have any more respect for him than he did for us. The bull turned on our grandpa and that made our grandpa extremely distressed. Grandpa went directly to his neighbors' house. They made some kind of an arrangement. I never knew the specifics. We had been anxious about our grandpa when he and the neighbor went to the barn. They assured us that they knew exactly what they were going to do .... and they did it .... and .... we ate him! [The bull not Grandpa].

We were never sure what our grandpa utilized for a bull when he needed one or what kind of an arrangement our grandpa had made with his neighbor. What we knew for sure was that the neighbor carted off a substantial portion of our grandpa's bull and the neighbor's bull always looked like he had a little smile on his face and he seemed to walk with a little more spring to his step.

Grandma and Grandpa Welch
Marcus & Cora Welch

My mother's parents were desceased before I was born so I never knew them, or much of anything about them. My mother had an older brother, Glenn, who was 17 years older than she and a sister, Pearl, who was about 14 years older. Her nieces and nephews were more her age than her siblings. Her sister, Kyra was 8 years younger. She died at the age of 20.

December 7, 1941

On December 7, 1941 the Japanese bombed Pearl Harbor and suddenly our country was at war. When the news bulletin came over the radio my mother was coming up the cellar stairs with a pan of potatoes. She dropped the potatoes to listen to the news bulletins as they came in. I remember her weeping and my father in tears as we were now at war and their oldest son, Bob, was in the army.

Our neighbors, Asel and Mildred Alysworth, came to our house that Sunday night, something that they almost never did. The talk was about the war and Bob being in the service and how glad they were that their son, Carl, who had just turned 15 wouldn't have to go and fight. Three years later, (December, 1944) Carl was killed at the Battle of The Bulge in Belgium.

My brother, Bob, had hit the beaches of France on D-Day, June 6, 1945 and fought the entire European operation from France to Luxembourg, to Belgium, to Germany and returned home after the war ended in Europe. He was in

Belgium when Hitler's troops broke through. The army had decided to march fresh, new troops to the front thus allowing the tired seasoned troops some rest, not knowing that the German Army was planning their last big offensive. Bob didn't know that his neighbor was being marched past him at the time. When Carl was killed, I was both sad and angry. Carl was about the nicest guy that I knew. I had always looked up to and admired Carl. He was kind of like another big brother, he always treated me right. War is always such a waste.

Times were difficult for everyone during the war. Gas, sugar, meat and other items were rationed and you needed ration stamps to purchase these items, if they were available. There were no such things as candy bars, or gum, or bananas, or any imported fruits during the war. The last cars built for retail were in 1941 and cars didn't get back on the market until 1946 and even then only a very few were produced. There was a black market for cars after the war and the government had to step in to stop it.

I Get A Kick Out Of Milking

In September of 1942, when I was ten years old, my parents had their 25th wedding anniversary. Bob was stationed on Governor's Island by New York City and they decided to take a Greyhound Bus to New York to visit him and to celebrate. My father had a cousin, Lester Fuller, who was almost 29 years old at the time. Lester peddled household products and often hired out to farmers to help do the milking and other chores. He was hired to run the farm for a few days.

We had a cow that just didn't like to be milked. She would kick and kick every time my father would try to milk her, so he bought a set of what we called "leg bracelets." They were in fact manacles for unruly cows. When he put the manacles on the cow's ankles, she couldn't kick anymore as her legs were hobbled. My father forgot to tell Lester about her. My sister, Pauline, and I were in the barn milking our cows. When Lester got to the kicking cow we just sort of snickered and sneaked a peek from behind the cows that we were milking to see what would happen. Lester no sooner sat down when his milk pail went sailing past me. I thought that that was the funniest thing that I had ever seen. Lester picked up his milk pail and tried it again, and again the milk pail went flying. We were laughing so hard at an unproductive Lester and the flying milk pail that he became a little agitated. He asked us if we were of the opinion that we could do the job any better. I let him know that I was a ten year old pro at milking cows and no cow was going to kick my milk pail around the barn. I marched over to the cow. The manacles were hanging by her stanchion so I reached up and put them on the cows ankles. I had never put the manacles on the cow before, but I had seen it done and I knew that it worked. I sat down with the milk stool and placed the pail on the extended rack very gently taking hold of the cow's teats. I surmise that perhaps I didn't have the manacles installed properly, because as soon as I touched the cow her hoof came up and caught me behind the neck and landed me face down in the manure gutter that was well supplied with fresh summer cow manure. Now Lester was doing the laughing. I ran from the barn and jumped into the cow's watering tub in the barn yard. After I changed my clothes and dried off, I went back into the barn and finished my chores. Every day, both in the morning and in the evening, Lester would invite me to milk that cow. I had learned the meaning of humiliation.

Lester joined the Army Air Corps in 1943 and I never saw him again until June of 1995, over 52 years later, when Lore and I looked him up. He was living near Cooperstown, NY and was 4 months short of being 82 years old. He was still peddling household products. I didn't mention the kicking cow to him. {Lester died on January 19, 1997 at the age of 83. He was the last of my Dad's cousins]

The Farm Is Sold

In the spring of 1943, when we returned home on the school bus, a farmer named Lysle Stanton and his son, John, were talking to my father. When they left we were told that they had made an offer to buy the farm. Johnny was working with his father on his farm, but he wanted to have his own farm. Farmers were exempted from the draft, if they had their own farm. We never really knew for sure if Johnny would really rather milk cows than shoot Nazi's and we never really cared. The one thing that we knew for sure was that we were going to get off the farm. My mother was happy. She had tasted village life and she was going to enjoy it again. I was happy for the same reason. I knew that my milking days were over. No more feeding the animals, no more filling silos, no more haying, no more cleaning the barn, no more gathering eggs, no more drudgery. We were going to be free of all that and live the good life. Sometimes things don't always work out the way that you think that they should.

My father took a job in a defense factory. We knew that we were going to be rich. Some of the factories were paying as much as 75 cents per hour, and with time and a half for overtime. We even heard of some people making over $100.00 in one week with their overtime pay. The only problem was, things were getting more expensive. Bread had gone up to 15 cents a loaf but, what the heck, my mother baked her own bread. Gasoline was almost 20 cents a gallon but again, what the heck, there wasn't any gasoline to buy anyhow.

We moved into a nice big house in the village. There were just three kids still at home. Not a cow to milk. Not a pig to feed. No hay to pitch. No barn to clean. Life just couldn't get much better. Pauline had a few rabbits. My mother kept a few hens in a small space in the back of the garage, behind which was a little chicken run. I had freedom.

We had real electricity. We had real running water. We had an indoor toilet. We had a bath tub. We had a refrigerator which had been converted from an ice box, but it was electric and it kept the food cold. I had been emancipated. I had freedom!

Freedom Lost

One day my father came home with what he thought was some really great news. He had learned that a paper route was available in the village of Edmeston and he had saved it just for me. Now wasn't that thoughtful. It didn't matter that I was only eleven years old and the paper bag dragged on the ground. The paper route covered the entire village and altogether it covered about a three mile radius. Papers were 3 cents each and I collected 18 cents a week from my customers. I had to carry a pocket full of pennies as no one in Edmeston had ever heard of tipping, especially tipping as much as 2 cents all at once. When the price of the paper went up to 4 cents, I had to collect 24 cents a week and still acquired no tips but I got blamed for the high cost of the newspapers. Later, I also obtained the morning paper route becoming the only daily paper boy in town. Eventually I took over the Sunday paper routes and became the only paper boy in town. I added to my income in the summers, by mowing lawns for 25 cents each using a hand push mower. I was never happier and, with the exception of having to fight the town bully a few times every week, I was doing okay. The fights went on for over a year until one day he beat me real bad. After that he never attacked me again. He just had to prove to all of the kids in the village that he was the toughest. If I had known that, I would have taken a beating on the first fight and would have had a peaceful year. I was learning to live like the town kids and a couple of paper routes were a breeze compared to farm work.

My father was homesick for the farm. He hated factory work. He rented a barn at the edge of the village and bought 10 cows as his first step back into farming.

I Learn How To Chew Tobacco

My father worked the night shift at the war factory, so I had to feed and milk the cows at night after I finished my paper route. My sister, Pauline, had agreed to do the milking but she was getting interested in boys and didn't like the idea of smelling like cows, so she got a job baby sitting.

The barn that my father rented was at the very end of North Street across the road from my last paper customer, so I could feed and milk the cows and then go home for supper. We had about eight cows milking at the time. I was now almost twelve years old and the barn had real electric lights, so it didn't seem like such a hard job. I hadn't forgotten how to milk cows. It's like riding a bike, you never forget how to do it. I had to learn how to hold the milk pail between my legs, as I no longer had my milk stool with the extension. It was the standard three legged milk stool.

My father had a couple of bad habits. One of them was chewing tobacco when he milked cows. He would chew a little. Milk a little. Spit a little. He was pretty good at not getting too much of it into the milk pail. One cold winter night after finishing my paper route, I went into the barn to start milking and realized that I was very hungry. With nothing in the barn to eat except hay and cow grain, I remembered that my father had his *Red Man* chewing tobacco in a little cupboard in the barn. I thought that maybe a little chew would ease the hunger. I opened the package and took a smell. It smelled pretty good so I took out a big chew and sat down to milk the first cow. Everything was great for a few minutes. I was chewing. I was milking. I was spitting. I was doing everything right. Suddenly the cows started going around in circles. I got the first cow milked, and started towards the milk house to empty the milk pail into the milk can, when the milk house started going around in circles. I finally got that under control and the next thing I knew the milk can was going around in circles. Pouring milk from a pail into a milk strainer and milk can that won't stay still is almost impossible. I soon realized that my boots were getting full. Somehow I got some of the milk into the milk can and started back to the barn. I realized that I was drunk on tobacco juice. I don't know if all of the cows got milked that night or not. The next morning my father was very disturbed and accused me of not doing my job. He seemed to think that some of the cows either were not milked at all, or that they weren't milked completely. He demanded to know, "where was all of the milk?" He knew that he had a short load of milk the next morning. He had a short temper too. I never attempted to chew tobacco again until I was in the 9th grade. That's another story.

More Tobacco—More Problems

We had a class in the 9th grade that was called Social Studies. This class covered everything from current events to history. Our teacher was a great guy named Charles Rider. He had a grand sense of humor but he did have his limits. One morning during class, a class mate named Guy Carey, Jr. pulled out a plug of *Honey Cut Chewing Tobacco*. It was tobacco pressed into a rectangle shape and you would bite off a chew as you felt the need or desire. Guy took a big bite and started to chew and passed it on to Gordy Fitch. Gordy passed in on to Ken Klingler. Ken passed it on to Al Higgins. Al Higgins passed it on to Al Riedel. Al passed it on to me. I took a bite and began to chew. Chewing tobacco is not to be swallowed even if it is flavored with honey. So the time came when Guy Carey, Jr. had to spit so he got up and walked out of class to the boys' room next door to our class room and spit. Soon the next guy left the room to rid himself of his burden, and he was followed by the next guy, and so on, until it came to my turn.

Mr. Rider stopped teaching and said that he didn't know what was going on, but "**No One but No One**," was to leave the room without permission. Well, it is hard to ask permission with your mouth full of *Honey Cut*; especially when it's kind of running out of the corners of your mouth. So I did the next best thing. I swallowed the chew, the juice along with it. This was the last morning class before lunch. I had eaten my chew for lunch and no longer wanted lunch. Permission or no permission I got out of my chair and headed for the boys' room. I didn't make it. I got as far as the door where I upchucked everything into the wastepaper basket. The first thing that went by was the *Honey Cut*. Next came breakfast, followed by last night's supper, and I think that I noticed my shoe laces flying past. I was drained, exhausted, sweating and dizzy, and the class room was one smelly mess. Mr. Rider said, "Fuller, you could have gone to the boys' room." He had to let the class out early and call the janitor to clean up the mess to try to eliminate the smell. You can't imagine how bad honey can smell when it is not properly recycled. I was allowed to return to class the next day. For the most part, we had some even-tempered and tranquil teachers back then.

I Learn Shorthand

Speaking of teachers, I'm prone to skip ahead a little to 1946. We were fortunate in Edmeston to have some very exemplary teachers and most were very tolerant. Mrs. Audry Lohnas taught me typing in the 10th grade. I was 14 years old when I started the 10th grade, and I thought that I was some real hot stuff. I earned a 96 on my NY State Regents Exam and hit 48 wpm [words per minute] on an old Woodstock manual typewriter that no one else in our class would use. I had no choice. The big guys naturally took the better machines, and even the girls were bigger than me. Consequently, I took whatever was remaining. The regents score and the 48 wpm beat the juniors and the seniors and I received an award at the end of the year that included a pin and a $5.00 bill, all presented to me at what was known as Class Night. (I still have the pin but I must have mislaid the $5.00 bill). The graduating class always had a class night shortly before graduation that was very well attended by the community. Mrs. Lohnas was so sure that she had a winner in me that she invited me to take Gregg Shorthand the following year. If there was a booby prize for shorthand, I would have easily come in first. I can still remember how to write "Dear Sir" in shorthand. That was my total achievement for that class. If this woman hadn't been so good-hearted and diligent, I would have surely failed my shorthand. But with a little stratagem and collaboration from this unusual teacher, I obtained a final average of 65, a passing grade, even though it wasn't what you would call a commendable scholastic rating. She had often said that she wondered what a boy could accomplish in her shorthand class. I showed her.

Don't Lick the Zipper

While I'm skipping ahead [or behind], I want to give everyone of you a word of advice.

Don't lick the zipper.

When I was in the seventh grade, our teacher was always very generous in her teachings regarding common sense things. We had been experiencing an extremely cold winter, and she felt that she should warn us about not doing stupid little things like sticking a hot tongue on cold metal. She went on to explain how the hot tongue would stick to the cold metal and that it was almost impossible to separate the two. We all found that to be a very interesting bit of information; but why would a teacher waste our time teaching us about such things that had so little value or effect on our young lives. Besides, who in their sane mind would do such a stupid thing anyhow?

That afternoon the temperature was near zero while I was delivering my newspapers. I was near the end of my route, and becoming somewhat bored with the cold weather and the delivery of newspapers my mind somehow diverted back to our science lesson. I had a very large tab on my jacket zipper, used to pull the zipper up or down. It occurred to me that occasionally teachers are wrong about certain things. For no good reason, I bent my head down and squarely placed my pudgy little tongue on that large and abundant tab. The teacher was flawless in her conjecture. I finished delivering the last few papers that evening with my head bent down and my tongue tightly fastened to my jacket zipper tab. When I returned home, my mother thought that the whole thing was hilarious. It took several minutes of pouring cold water over my tongue and the jacket tab before I was liberated.

Another Farm

My father couldn't stand working in the factory and he missed his farming. In 1944 he bought a farm about a mile out of the village, and only about a mile from the big farm where I was born. It wasn't as large as the big farm (about 125 acres), but the barn was big enough for 25 to 30 cows. My mother stood her ground. She was not moving onto any farm again. She loved the village and so did us three remaining kids. This meant that the farm house would remain empty, so my father filled the farmhouse with rabbits. There was a war on and everything was rationed, even meat, so selling rabbit meat should be very profitable. My father started with just a few rabbits…but rabbits multiply like…well…like rabbits. Every room soon had rabbits. The kitchen had rabbits. The dining room had rabbits. The three bedrooms had rabbits. The rabbits had rabbits. We had rabbit for Sunday dinner. We had rabbit for lunch. We had rabbit for supper. We had rabbit stew. We had rabbit pot pie. We had rabbit soup. We had rabbit fried. We had rabbit boiled. We had rabbit roasted. We had rabbit fur. Rabbit mittens. Rabbit jackets. Rabbit ear muffs. Rabbit hand muffs. We had rabbits "FOR SALE." We had rabbits "FOR FREE." We even put an ad in the Edmeston Local Newspaper at Christmas time. "**Give the gift that keeps on giving, pregnant rabbits for sale.**" Nothing worked. Not too many people in town liked to eat rabbit, and it took awhile for my father to realize that rabbits don't lay eggs and they don't give milk. They do give manure.

My father had a chance to sell the farm and buy a smaller farm at the edge of the village. The new owner was going to live in the house so the house had to be cleaned up. My father and I shoveled and spread rabbit manure for days. We shoveled rabbit manure out of the kitchen. We shoveled rabbit manure out of the dinning room. We shoveled rabbit manure out of the living room. We shoveled rabbit manure out of the bedrooms. I shoveled rabbit manure in my sleep. I never want to see another rabbit. I get hopping mad just thinking about rabbits.

One Last Move

It was 1945, I was now 13 years old and the war had ended, when my father sold the farm and the big house on North

Street, and bought a small farm on the edge of the village. Actually, the house was in the village. The farm extended from behind the barn and chicken houses which might also have been considered to be in the village. There was no zoning so that didn't matter. My mother, my sisters and I were all happy to still be in the village. My father had his farm, albeit a very small farm.

The barn had wooden floors, calf pens, hog pens and stanchions for only two cows. Before we could ship milk, it was required that we have a cement floor in the barn. This took us several days. I shoveled the cement, sand and gravel, poured water into the cement mixer, and my father would dump the mixed cement into a wheel barrow and push it into the barn where he had two men working the cement. We, as a matter of fact, remade the barn. Now we were ready to ship milk. But the barn was too small to keep more than about a dozen cows. The other buildings, including the second floor of the horse barn, and miscellaneous chicken and hen houses, had space for only about two or three hundred hens, so my father worked on the State Road, from time, to time, to supplement his income.

In the spring of 1947, one of our horses came down with a disease called the heaves and had to be destroyed. The other horse was getting along in years, so they were both sold to the glue factory. The war was over, farm tractors were being produced again, and we were able to purchase a small

Farmall tractor. I went to the dealer after school, picked up the tractor and proudly drove it home. My father used that tractor for over 30 years.

The Entrepreneur

My father was working full time on the road, which left him very little time to work the farm. Cleaning the barn and spreading the manure was very time consuming. The farm was so small that we couldn't use all of the manure. We were accumulating a considerable pile out back of the barn. There was an exceptional demand for cow manure around the village. People wanted it spread on their gardens. I made a deal with my father. I could sell the manure for $1.00 a load. I had to deliver and spread it, but the dollar was mine to keep. There was one big disadvantage. For every load that I sold in the village, I had to spread one for my father on the farm. It took me a couple of years, of loading and spreading, before I realized that I was really spreading two loads for a dollar but, even at that, it was clear profit. I knew that I would have to spread my father's manure anyhow.

One Inconsolable Customer

It's hard to believe, but I had one customer that was never satisfied with my manure. He was a retired school superintendent named, Prof. Thayer. This man was always dressed in a three piece suit and tie, even though he was around 80 years old and had been retired for many years. He would follow me to his garden, in his suit and tie, and instruct me as to how he wanted the manure spread. I have to tell you, this old guy was as spry as a fox. No matter how many times I gave the manure fork a little extra effort, when I pitched the manure toward him, he somehow always got out of the way. He would complain to my father, not about my attempt to hit him with the manure, but that I wasn't bringing a big enough load for his dollar. My father would make me bring the old guy another load for free.

One day when he called for his annual manure event, I told him that the cows had been terribly constipated and that we didn't have any manure to spare. Prof. Thayer contacted my father. My father contacted me. After a surly little consultation with my father, I ascertained that perhaps there had been a mix up and, somehow, I located a rather substantial pile of manure. My father was not happy with me and he judged that it might be a splendid idea for me to deliver two loads to the old Prof. for **free**.

Although I have never been certain, I think, with painstaking aim and considerable resolve, I got the old guy when I delivered the second load. He never bothered me again. I surmise he decided that he wasn't taking any more *manure* from me.

My Father— The Church Sexton

Working on the road took up to much of my father's time, so he acquired a part-time job as the Church Sexton (janitor) at the Baptist Church. It worked out very well. The pay was small, but the hours were flexible, and he could clean the church and ring the bells on Sunday morning without it interfering with his regular farm chores. The bells were to be tolled one hour before services and as they were high up in the steeple they could be heard for a great distance. My father kept this job for many years, until one night when he got his schedule a little mixed up.

It seems that he had been cavorting with some of his friends at the Gaskin house (the local pub) one Saturday night and, somehow, time had slipped away. They closed the bar at 3:00 A.M. and sent my father home.

As he was making his way up North Street towards home, he had to go past the Baptist Church. He remembered that he had to ring the bells for Sunday services. Something that he had consumed seemed to be clouding his mind. He wasn't just sure as to exactly what time it was, but knew that the bells had to be rung, and remembered that it was Sunday morning. Without deliberating, he took out the church keys, opened the door and climbed to the bell tower and found the familiar bell rope.

For some reason the townspeople not being accustomed to bells ringing at 3:00 A.M., seemed to think that there might be some kind of an emergency and that, perhaps, the village fire alarm was not working. So they began to gather at the church.

When my father finally made it down from the belfry but was unable to explain his actions to their satisfaction, the preacher, who lived next door to the church, was the first to approach him and informed him that he was fired.

My father told me that it was a little degrading to be relieved of his position in this way. He said that he thought that, perhaps, the reason that the preacher was so unsettled was that he didn't have a sermon ready, and that he had never had so many people out to church before, especially so early in the morning.

My parents stayed on the little farm to their dying day. Because the church had withheld Social Security, they were eligible for, and commenced collecting Social Security at about the same time that my father lost the church job. He continued to milk cows and keep his hens until he was 75 years old when he finally totally retired.

THREE

The Juvenile Delinquent

I had saved several dollars when I had the opportunity to buy a second hand 22 single shot rifle with a telescope sight. I loved that rifle, and often found time to go woodchuck hunting and later used it for hunting squirrel and other game. Nothing was sacred. One day I was woodchuck hunting with a friend, Dick Rollins, and we were about 300 yards from a swamp when we spotted a cat sneaking up on something. Dick proposed that I could never hit that cat from that distance but I insisted that I could. I attempted to prove it. I set my sights, took my aim and pulled the trigger. The bullet went "zing" just behind the stalking cat, apparently hitting a stone instead of the cat. That cat was so frightened that it jumped straight into the air, pounced on the stone with real determination, looked at it and then ran away at breakneck speed as fast as his four legs would carry him. We laughed so hard that we ached.

One day a couple of us boys went to visit a classmate at his home on a farm, taking along our rifles. We settled on a great idea. This farmer was plagued with annoying pigeons.

Pigeons make a terrible mess and contaminating the hay in the hay loft with their droppings. We knew that we would be appreciated if we could rid the barn of these pesky pigeons. We went into the hay loft and shot several birds before we went home. We heard later from our friend that his father couldn't understand why his barn roof suddenly started to leak every time that it rained. It had never leaked before.

One pleasant, sunny Sunday afternoon when I was 13 years old, on the 16th of September 1945, Red Benson and I went for a walk along Wharton Creek that flowed between Edmeston and West Burlington. We had our rifles and were shooting at fish and mud turtles along the way. Suddenly it started to rain. We raced for an old abandoned cider mill. The windows were all busted out so we crawled inside to keep dry. While in the cider mill, we noticed several large wooden barrels full of empty glass bottles. To this day I don't know why glass bottles were in the cider mill as no one put cider in glass bottles, they used wooden barrels. While waiting for it to stop raining, we decided to set some of the bottles up on the beams and using them for target practice. We had a great time. It stopped raining and we left.

We had had such a good time with target practice that we went back the next Sunday afternoon, for more of the same. Bringing along Fuzzy Burdick, we finished off the remaining bottles, went home, and that was that. Or so we thought.

On the 4th of October, when I came home from peddling my papers, there was a New York State Trooper in the living room by the name of P.R.Vandermark with a summons for Raymond Fuller to appear in Children's Court, Otsego County on the 9th day of October at 11:00 o'clock. The three of us were charged with breaking and entering (which we didn't do as the windows were already broken) and also charged with breaking several windows and "valuable" personal property. At children's court we tried to explain to the judge that there weren't any windows to break; that we, simply crawled into the cider mill through the already broken windows. He would not listen to us. We admitted to having been there. We admitted to having shot up some bottles. We had no defense. The owner of the cider mill, Irwin Stevens, said that we did the damage and that was that. We were directed to pay for damages. The sum of $75.00 doesn't sound like much in today's dollars, but it was a fortune in 1945. Because Red and I had been there twice we had to pay $30.00 each and Fuzzy had to pay $15.00. If we paid the damages then all charges would be dropped and we could go home. We made arrangements to pay and went home.

We later found out [and they admitted it] that three or four other boys that also lived in the village, but were from more "*prominent*" families, had broken into the cider mill and broken the windows all out, a couple of weeks before Red and I came upon it. Justice is swift. No one ever said that it's fair.

My Motorbike

My brother-in-law, Russell Ripley, was handy with tools. He could fix it or he could build it. In 1947, he took a balloon tire, girls' bike and attached a Briggs-Stratten gasoline engine to it. The engine was an old washing machine motor. Most farmers didn't have electricity so used gasoline motors to run various appliances, including washing machines.

He rigged it up with a pulley clutch, a hand throttle, gas tank, the works. The brakes were on the peddles. The bike was designed to go no more than 20 to 25 miles per hour at top speed. This was the greatest thing that I had ever seen. It was loud but it was fast. I just had to have it. I had saved up $100 from my paper routes, so I made an offer and he accepted. I now had wheels. Real wheels. I used it to peddle papers with. I used it to go up and down the streets of Edmeston. I used it to drive people almost crazy. I went everywhere with it. My mother was driving home one day in her 1936 Chrysler driving a hardy 50 miles per hour and I passed her. When I would get that thing over 35 miles per hour it would shimmy and shake the living day lights out of me. My arms and head would shake unmercifully. I would bestow a generous grin with my bug stained teeth and dispense a happy face to everyone along the way.

Some people thought that maybe I was a little demented. Some people thought that I was a nuisance. Some people thought that I shouldn't be on the road. Some even thought that it might be good if I was run out of town. I had no license. The bike wasn't registered. Getting rid of me became a preoccupation with some people. Some ninny called the State Police.

I had heard a very unpleasant rumor that the State Police were in town looking for me. It turned out not to be a rumor. The State Police were in town with one goal in mind. That goal was to rid the town of loud noise Raymond. I spotted the troopers, and the troopers spotted me, just as I started up East Street. I calculated that the school parking lot was a better avenue of escape than the main road, and I guided by bike in that direction. They followed. With no problem at all, I zipped between the posts at the edge of the parking lot that were set 3 feet apart. The State Police couldn't get through. I went around the school and down the front side walk that brought me out onto North Street. The State Police had to turn around and go back to the four corners to come up North Street. I had the jump on them. I accelerated that bike up North Street as fast as it would go and had plenty of time to drive it to the rear of the horse barn. I shut it off, tossed an old buffalo robe over it to hide it, walked out of the barn and started down the street. The troopers had gone past our house and were coming back down North Street very slowly. They pulled up next to me and asked if I had seen the kid with the motorbike. I said, "What's a motorbike?" They looked at me kind of suspiciously. They looked at each other and one of them asked me if I had a motorbike. Again, I said, 'What's a motorbike?" They looked at each other, rolled their eyes and drove off.

If the New York State Police ever stop you to ask you if you have seen the kid with the noisy motorbike, whatever you do, don't tell them that it was me. Deny that you know the kid with the motorbike, they may just look at you kind of peculiar, but hopefully they will drive away.

The Mooning of The Baptists

We had a neighbor that lived across the street who had a game leg and walked with a real bad limp. Everyone called him Step and a Half. His real name was Worthy Chase. He was a very kind and patient old man and every one liked him. He also had a Model A Ford coupe with a rumble seat. One day Worthy came home for lunch and dropped dead. [Some lunches are better than others.]

My friend, Red Benson, bought Worthy's Model A Ford.

One bright and beautiful Sunday morning in January, shortly after I had turned 16 years old, Red stopped at the house and picked me up for a ride around the country. It had snowed the night before and some of the back roads had virgin snow on them and we were going to break tracks.

It was always very pretty before the snow plows spoiled it. The one problem we had was the fact that Red had already picked up four other guys. He had two in the front seat with him and two in the rumble seat in the back.

In case you don't know what a rumble seat is let me tell you. You don't really want to ride in one in the winter. You don't want to ride in one when it rains. You don't want to ride in one when it's hot and dusty. In fact most people didn't ever want to ride in one because you sat outdoors. The seat was where a trunk would be on a car. It just opened from the top and exposed a small seat where the passengers were exposed to the elements.

With the car full, I had no seat so I stepped on the running board on the driver's side and off we went. We drove to some back roads, went past woods with trees heavy with pure white snow and on past several farms. Even though my posterior was getting a little cold, we were having a great time until we broke over a knoll and started down a hill with no idea where the road was. Everything was white. Red guessed where the road might be. Red guessed wrong. We were headed for a fenced in pasture. The fence was barbed wire. My back side was sticking out somewhat as I had my head inside the car to keep it warm, when, without warning, I felt a sharp tug on the seat of my britches. I also felt a stinging sensation and some very cold air where cold air shouldn't be.

I had lost the seat of my pants, and part of my own seat, to the barbed wire fence.

Somehow we got out of the pasture. I told Red that I had to get home right away because I was hurt and bleeding a little and I had also lost a good part of my pants. We headed directly for home but we had to go through the village. We went up North Street just as the Baptist Church was letting out. I stuck my head inside the car, as far as possible, so that no one would recognize me, and the only thing facing the Baptists, as we went by, was my exposed behind. I don't know how they knew that it was me that went flying past riding on the running board of Red's Model A Ford, but someone did, because it was all over town that I had *mooned* the Baptist worshipers on Sunday morning.

My mother was very upset with me. Nevertheless, she wanted to be sure that I didn't get an infection so out came the iodine. Wow! She emptied the bottle on my open sores and I yelped like a kicked dog but, I guess that, it worked. I healed up back there, but I didn't have it so easy in the village explaining my Sunday morning behavior. My mother took some heat from the neighbors as she tried to explain what had happened, but no one wanted to hear our side of the story. I had mooned the Baptists as they were leaving church, and that was that. To prove my story, I even offered to show several of the ladies my injuries but they said they didn't want to lower themselves to that. To them, I was a mooner. It didn't matter to anyone that a considerable and important part of my pants were hanging on some farmer's barbed wire fence, just blowing in the wind as a warning to other motorists that "**The Road Ends Here.**"

No One Likes A Wise Guy

Some of us guys thought that it would be great sport and very funny if we put a cinder block under the transmission of our Ag teacher's car. We knew that Mr. Vrooman, our teacher, had a good sense of humor and that he would probably think that this was a great and funny thing to do. We rounded up enough guys to lift the car and slid the block underneath. Of course, when the teacher tried to drive his car it wouldn't move. We had our laugh and we, like the heroes that we were, went to help the poor guy out. Being very brilliant, we figured out the problem for him and quickly solved it. The teacher was extremely grateful to us, until one of our class mates told him who was responsible for this depraved stunt.

This did not sit well with us boys and this poor guy received the nickname of "Stooly." Every time one of us got into trouble, proof or no proof, Stooly got the blame. I don't know if it was ever proven that Stooly was the actual culprit or not, but we had reason to believe that he was, so he was going to have to pay for his transgression.

One day I received a catalog that advertised some grand tricks to pull on people. One advertisement displayed a picture of a man with his face all black, the result of an exploding cigar. It also pictured people taking a piece of their special gum and immediately running to the bathroom, from the laxative in the gum. It pictured a car with smoke and a loud bang, the unsuspecting driver frightened nearly to death. I thought that these were about the neatest tricks that I had ever seen and I ordered some of each.

The Exploding Cigar

Occasionally, I found myself in the principal's office. On one of my trips, I noted that the principal smoked cigars. I made a mental note of this and on my next trip, I made an even exchange of one of my exploding cigars for one of his, before he had time to meet me at his interrogation room. I made the mistake of boasting to my comrades what I had done. I was told that Stooly had gone to the principal and had informed him of my mischief. Apparently some one had. I was invited to meet the principal in his office without delay.

I knew that I was in for a real dressing down and maybe even a bonus on top of that. We called it *physical therapy*, he called it the rubber hose. [More on that later].

Entering his office I saw laid out on his desk my cigar, sliced lengthwise and exposed was a spring contraption held by a string that was supposed to burn and release the spring when one lit the cigar. The principal, instead of being incensed, was really very impressed. He told me that he had had a small problem with his own cigars. Often, he noticed that a cigar or two would come up missing and, even though he was quite certain who was taking them, he thought that maybe he would teach the culprit a lesson. He wanted to know if I had any more exploding cigars as he wanted to buy a couple. I sold him my entire stock, allowing myself a small margin of profit.

He never reported to me the outcome of his experiment. We did notice a that couple of teachers had dark colors on the end of their noses, but we were never certain what it was or from where it came.

The Exploding Car

I just knew that I had a winner with the car bombs. I had had some fun watching some of my friends nearly pass out when they thought their car had met its doom.

One Friday night our science teacher, Mr. DuMont, had driven several of the high school girls to the roller-skating rink. While they were in the rink, I enlisted the aid of a couple of my friends, and we installed a bomb under the hood of his car. When he attempted to start the car, it began to smoke and whistle very loudly ending in a tumultuous *BOOM*. The girls were screaming, Mr. DuMont was struggling to get his car hood up and we were laughing our heads off. It would have ended there, but the teacher found out who the culprits were and the reprimand wasn't so funny. I was told that it was Stooly who had told the teacher whom the mischievous villains were.

I really began to detest this guy.

The Laxative Chewing Gum

I wondered to whom I should give the laxative gum. Who could be better than a guy that you want to get even with. I led the poor guy to believe that all was forgiven and we should be pals, showing my sincerity by offering him a couple of pieces of gum. In fact, I offered him several pieces and watched him chew my special gift. I had let several other guys in on the joke, and we all sat around waiting for poor Stooly to make his mad dash to the crapper. Nothing happened. Later, I gave him some more and he chewed that too. Nothing happened.

Knowing that the gum didn't work, we decided to chew the stuff ourselves. I had purchased a large supply as my intentions were not really virtuous. We all enjoyed the chewing gum. Several of us shared the gum but nothing happened to any of us. No one had to go to the privy. I was sure that I had been ripped off.

Dick Rollins lived almost across the street from me. Behind his house was the Mill Creek and his father had built a narrow foot bridge across the creek where they had a shanty. Dick and I often were allowed to camp out in the shanty and this was one of those nights. Since the gum hadn't done anything for us in the afternoon, we decided to finish it up. So we chewed several pieces before going to bed.

About 2:00 A.M. I heard a rustling from the other bed and the door burst open, I saw a figure running toward the house and I was hot on his tail. That stuff was working now. We couldn't make it to the house. We were both doubled over, clinging onto the edge of the foot bridge, while our very life was flowing away from us into Mill Creek at an extremely high velocity. The pace at which the creek was rising was alarming.

Dick and I wobbled to school the next day and found that several boys were absent. It seems that there was an epidemic of diarrhea going around. The school nurse was alarmed at the number of boys, and yet no girls, that had caught this unusual torment. *I made a note to myself to be certain to invite the girls to our next banquet.*

The Sabotaged Pipe

Mr. Rider, our Social Studies teacher, kept his smoking pipe in his middle desk drawer, fully packed with his favorite tobacco, so he could run down to the boiler room and grab a few quick puffs between classes. He also kept a box of white chalk in the same drawer. The chalk came packed in sawdust. We knew that it would be great amusement for us if we could mix a little sawdust with his pipe tobacco. One day opportunity came knocking when Mr. Rider left the room, for reasons we didn't know or care. With one of the guys acting as lookout, I went to the desk and emptied the pipe tobacco out of the pipe, replacing it with sawdust and putting a covering of tobacco on the top. We then anticipated the fun when the poor guy would likely find his smoke rather tasteless, and wonder if maybe he just might be better off giving up smoking.

We never had our fun. Someone tipped him off. The intelligence segment of our class, reported that Stooly had performed the despicable deed, spoiling our entertainment.

Make Love, Not War

During the lunch recess, I accused Stooly of doing this appalling thing and we got into a rather nasty little fight. I was giving more than I was taking, when we were abruptly pulled apart by our gym coach. We had only one coach in the school. He was both coach and gym teacher, and taught everything that had to do with gym and sports including baseball, basketball and football. He made some remark about "so you like to fight," but nothing more was said and he sent us back to our homeroom.

The first class after lunch was gym. The coach decided that today we would learn how to wrestle. He announced to the class that Ray Fuller liked to fight and that he was sure I could teach the class a few things. He deposited me on the wrestling mat with a kid that looked massive to me. Never having wrestled before we both ended up off the mat. The coach claimed that I was first off the mat so my husky opponent could take an advantage. I was to get on my hands and knees, the other *apprentice* could take any hold that he wanted, and at the whistle we were to start wrestling. The other young man didn't know how to wrestle either and we ended up off the mat again. I had to get back on my hands and knees again, but this time the coach was going to show the class how to benefit from the advantage. I was in position as the coach stepped in explaining to the class just how this hold that he had on me would easily win the match. He blew his whistle and not knowing what do, I guess I did the wrong thing, somehow I pinned the coach to the cheers of the entire gym class. That ended our wrestling classes. *The next year he took a coaching job in Oneonta, NY. I told every one that he was scared of me.*

Lesson Time

The next day when I arrived at the school, I walked into the gym as I often did before class. I noticed that the school janitors were installing a boxing ring. I had never seen a boxing ring before. I had never seen a boxing glove or a boxing match. We didn't have television in those days, and the only thing that I knew about boxing was that Joe Louis was the heavyweight champion of the world. Even my father would stay up to listen to one of his fights on the radio.

During Ag class it was announced over the loud speaker that there would be an assembly at 1:00 P.M. I thought "Good, no gym today." I thought wrong. The class was interrupted when the gym teacher came into the room with his "*roster*" of boxers for the assembly at 1:00 P.M.

He had paired up several of us boys, that he really didn't cherish, with some bigger and heavier guys. He was sure that he could teach us all a very valuable lesson by us getting our brains knocked out (legally). None of us had ever had a lesson in boxing and we were to put on a show for the entire school…and the first to box would be Ray Fuller verses "Squirt" Wilkinson. He was called Squirt because he was short but he was solidly built. Squirt was a couple of years older than me and about 25 pounds heavier. The 25 pounds was muscle. Your puny Grandpa had no choice but to fight Squirt in the ring, in front of the entire school. Having never seen a boxing glove before, I wasn't sure if I could lift my arm with that thing tied to the end of it. We were called to the center of the ring, given instructions of some kind and sent back to our corners. Some darn jerk rang a bell and we were told to come out fighting. Not knowing what to do, I walked up to Squirt and placed a commanding right to the side of his head and he went down with a hard thud. I was told to go to my own corner and I did. But when I turned around there was Squirt with his own impressive right to my chin and your paltry, pathetic Grandpa went flying over the top rope and out of the ring, to the howls and laughter of both the student and teacher body of the school.

I managed to crawl back into the ring on my hands and knees. I came up fighting mad. We were scheduled for three one minute rounds, but I was going to finish this guy off in seconds. I guess that Squirt had the same idea as we really got into a slugging contest and I wondered if someone had killed the bell ringer. I was convinced that the bell would never ring and I was going to have to clobber this guy throughout the rest of my life. It finally did ring, and I managed to stagger back to my corner where I intended to stay for the rest of my existence. I knew that my life would be short if I went back into that ring with Squirt. I heard a ringing in my ears and I was pushed back into the ring. I, all at once, realized that I was completely exhausted. With those lead weights called boxing gloves still tied to the end of my arms, I couldn't lift either arm. I looked across the ring at

Squirt and realized that I wasn't the only one staggering. We just meandered around looking at each other for one full minute with the school assembly giving us all the "booooos" that they could conjure up. They wanted another performance like round one. We were both exhausted and the third round went no better. We kind of held each other up for one full minute, so the coach called it a draw and sent us to the showers. We were allowed to watch the rest of the so called boxing matches, and were happy to realize that we were not the only ones to have been made to look like imbeciles by our gym teacher.

Smoking the Peace Pipe

[or a reasonable facsimile]

That night, being a Friday, was roller skating night in West Burlington. I had never seen Squirt at the skating rink before but there he was. I wasn't sure if he was there to finish me off or just there to roller skate. He came over to me and said, "You really hurt me with that first punch but I think that I got even, so let's be friends." That sounded good to me. He asked me to wait while he went across the street to a little store. Returning with a box of six little Italian cigars, he said to me, "Let's have a cigar." I had never smoked a cigar. I had chewed tobacco with some fairly negative results but a cigar was new to me. On top of that, I had never seen anything like these little flat, black, short and crooked things. We lit up. I soon realized what smoking old smelly, sweat socks wrapped in tar paper would taste like. Neither of us would dare inhale. It would mean sudden death for sure. We puffed and we blew smoke, and were both getting very sick, very fast but neither of us would put down our cigar until it was finished. Squirt offered me another. With a multitude of skaters watching the challenge we were facing, we lit up again. We both finished a second cigar. I was getting very sick but I accepted a third cigar.

Squirt didn't make it to the end of his third cigar. He suddenly ran out the front door and threw up over the top of a couple of parked cars. I think that he was socially embarrassed and saying nothing more, got in his car and left.

I received some good humor congratulatory backslapping from the other kids. I didn't need any backslapping. Now it was my turn to throw up and I did; all over the skating rink floor. The owner, lacking any sense of humor, made me clean up my mess and sent me home, disgraced and humiliated.

The Meanest Father

I was 10 years old in the summer of 1942 and my cousin Stuart Rood was 15. I always enjoyed staying at the Rood's as it was always a nice change from home. Usually, I didn't have to do any work as Stuart was required to do the work at his home.

The summer of 1942 was different. The war was on and most of the young men had enlisted or were being drafted into the military. Uncle Elbert's hired man had enlisted in the army and so he needed help haying. I thought that it was just the nicest thing when my mother said that I could stay at the Rood's for two or three weeks. I knew that I was needed at home but they let me go anyhow. As it turned out, it wasn't to be any kind of a vacation. I had been hired out to drive the team of horses for the haying season.

Uncle Elbert had several more modern tools than we had. He had a side delivery rake and a hay loader. The side delivery rake would rake the hay into, what we called, windrows. By straddling the windrows with the wagon, the hay loader attached to the rear of the wagon would pick up the hay and, like an elevator, it would deliver the hay into the wagon. I would drive the horses straddling the windrows and Uncle Elbert and Stuart would build the load. This was easy to do. I just had to keep my eyes on the windrows of hay and steer the horses to straddle them. The problem was, Stuart had raked the hay, and not thinking, he had raked one of the windrows under an apple tree. I didn't notice the apple tree as I was watching the windrow. Since the hay loader was taller than the wagon and I didn't notice the tree, there was a loud crash and the hay loader was all bent out of shape. So was Uncle Elbert. I just knew that I was in for a real bad time with my Uncle Elbert. I expected him to start yelling at me. He didn't. He was bawling out Stuart. Stuart should have known better than to rake the hay under the apple tree. It wasn't my fault that the hay loader was broken, it was Stuart's fault, and Stuart got the tongue lashing that I was convinced he deserved. Now if I had done this at home, I knew that I would have been in for a bad confrontation for being so simpleminded as to drive a team of horses with a wagon and hay loader under an apple tree, but Uncle Elbert took all of his wrath out on his inane son, Stuart.

That afternoon when Uncle Elbert was in town getting parts to repair the hay loader, Stuart started to pick on me for being so asinine. He said that he wished that my father was his father because my father was nicer than his father. I told him that my father was meaner than his father. That made him mad at me and he said that his father was a lot meaner than my father, and we got into a fight over who's father was the meanest. He took me down and stuffed grass into my mouth until I would acknowledge that his father was meaner than my father.

I don't know if Stuart got paid for working that summer, but that Mean Old Uncle Elbert paid me $3.00 for the 3 weeks that I worked and he didn't make me pay for the hay loader. $3.00 doesn't sound like much money today, but in 1942 it bought a new pair of shoes and I had a dollar left to buy a new pair of dungarees. The dungarees, back then, were a little different than those you buy today. Back in 1942 they were made of something like blue canvas and were held together with thread and brass rivets. They wore like iron and they felt like iron. When they developed a hole we could just patch them up. In those days my mother would darn the wool socks and patch up the cotton socks. Those darn socks would hurt your feet from the patching or the darning but everyone was in the same situation. We all had socks that were darned or patched. We all had pants that were patched. But only I had the meanest Uncle.

I Get a New Name

You will remember that back on the big farm my middle name was "*Go to The House*." In the village it was changed by the school teachers to "*Go To The Office*." I think that I spent more time in the office than the principal did and some of the kids even called me "Prof." My first experience was in the 5th grade. Some of us boys thought it great entertainment to chase a certain girl around the play ground. Somehow her dress became rather muddy and muddy dresses are not popular with teachers, mothers or principals.

The word was out, by the time that I arrived at school the next morning, that several 5th grade boys were to be invited to the principal's office to receive the rubber hose.

The principal's name was George Purple. Mr. Purple was a handsome man, very highly regarded and somewhat intimidating, as he had a way of looking right through you as if you were an open book. He could put the fear of God into you faster than a Baptist preacher. He also had two rubber hoses. Mr. Purple was a fair man. When you were going to receive the rubber hose you usually were warned in advance, so that you could have time to think about it. He also usually gave you a choice of the thick one that hurt like a day in purgatory, or the thin one that stung like a bumblebee. Also, when you went into his office for your "*interview*," the hoses were always placed on the table in full view so that you would have time to consider which one you were going to choose. What could be more fair than that.

I was way ahead of George Purple. Knowing that we were going to get the hose, I had stuffed several pieces of writing tablet cardboard into the seat of my pants to offset any pain that might be associated with a rubber hose of any description. After we had our little discourse with Mr. Purple, we were sent outside of the office into the waiting room. We were invited, one at a time, back into the office for our "*therapy*."

We could hear the boys ahead of us getting the hose which kind of made us a little nervous, but I wasn't too worried as I was prepared. The difficulty I had was that when I was invited to bend over onto the table to further my "*education*," the cardboard didn't bend. You might say, "*that it didn't go with the flow*."

I think that perhaps, 3 pieces were probably too many. Mr. Purple caught on very fast and the cardboard had to be removed before the performance could be concluded. The cardboard remained on his table for several days for all to see. We were put on notice that you can't fool George Purple.

How Much Can a Teacher Take

In the 7th grade we had a new Art teacher. Being young and inexperienced, some of the boys took advantage of her and fooled around in her class. One day, when we all felt in a very frisky mood and she was having a real bad time with us, she completely lost her cool. She was standing behind me when I said something that she apparently didn't like. I had hair in those days and she clamped onto it and yanked me out of my seat by my hair. She started to scream something and suddenly let go with a fist to my face. After that she lost all control and continued to strike me until my blood was all over my shirt. She then sent me to the boy's room to clean up. I looked a mess. I went home for lunch and my mother thought that I had been in another fight. I never told her anything different. I had a black eye, a bloody nose, and cuts and bruises all over my face. I was confident that if my mother knew that teacher had done that to me that she, my mother, would have blackened the other eye. The attitude in those days was if you got it from the teacher, you must have had it coming. And you probably did!

Making Points With the English Teacher

In high school, I was convinced that the English teacher, Mrs. Millie Miner, wasn't devotedly attached to me. She was young, and **we thought** inexperienced, but she didn't take any nonsense from anyone. She seemed to enjoy sending me to the principal's office, a whole lot more than I enjoyed going there. It seemed like it was "*go to the office*" for almost everything. Silly little things like falling asleep in my chair. I had the chair propped against the wall and after falling asleep, I hit the floor with a tremendous crash. I jumped up startled and looked around to see where I was. Sure enough, I was in English class and soon on my way to the principal's office.

One day, I made a "*scholarly*" remark in class about a poem that we had to learn. She advised me that I couldn't come back to class until I had written, "I will not talk in class 200 times." The next day when I came to class, I handed in a sheet of paper with "I will not talk in class 200 times" written across the top. She failed to see the humor in that. After another social call with the principal, it was decided that I not only would complete the original assignment but I would now do it twice.

Back in class, "Open your Prose and Poetry Books to page 237." "Today we are going to read the story, *Spreading The News*." I said, *"You mean Spreading The Manure."*

"Go to the office."

It seems that the principal had a better sense of humor than my English teacher, because when I related the incident to him he broke out laughing and to his dying day we shared a secret. He made me promise that if anyone asked if I received the rubber hose that I would say I had. He just couldn't bring himself to punish a farm kid for "*Spreading the Manure.*"

Book Reports

English class required that we read books and do book reports, both written and oral. I really didn't enjoy reading, and a book report was my most dreaded assignment. I was given the assignment of reading Moby Dick and was to have both a written report and an oral report ready to give on Monday. I figured that I could skim the book enough over the weekend to make some kind of a report; but hadn't figured on one of the older boys in the village named Ed Bailey, Jr. wanting me to go hunting with him. I told him that I had to read Moby Dick. He said not to worry, that he would tell me all about the book while we were hunting, since he had done a report on it when he was in the 9th grade. So I went hunting with Ed Bailey, Jr. instead of reading the book.

Ed Bailey, Jr. related the story to me. On Monday I was called on to give my oral report on Moby Dick and reported the story, just as it was told to me by my older hunting friend.

Moby Dick
The Ed Bailey, Jr. version

Moby Dick by Herman Melville. Moby Dick is a story about a great detective named Moby. Moby worked for Scotland Yard in England with a partner named Dr. John Watson. Together they became the most famous crime solving detectives ever to be known in England...*and I continued the story as it was told to me.*

For some reason, our English teacher didn't think that I had read the book and sent me to the principal's office with my written report. The principal agreed with the teacher that maybe I should reread the book and, also, it might not be a bad idea for me to read a couple of other books along with Moby Dick, and give the reports to him. One book, on his required reading list that I was to report to him on, was Sherlock Holmes by Sir Arthur Conan Doyle. It took a while but I did get the books read.

Was that Ed Bailey, Jr. ever mixed up. He didn't know the difference between a detective and a whale.

Historical note: Before Ed Bailey, Jr. and I went hunting that Sunday morning, he invited me to his house for a snack. He made us some toast. This is where I discovered the most marvelous thing that I had ever seen. Ed put the bread in the toaster and in a few moments it popped up toasted on both sides. I had never seen, or even heard of, a pop up toaster before. I knew that Ed Bailey, Sr. had to be one of the most important men in four counties to own an appliance like this one. My mother had acquired an electric toaster after the war but it had little doors on each side and you placed the bread on the door and closed it. After a few moments you opened the door, turned the bread over and toasted the other side. With experience, one could toast bread without burning it. I think that we called those few people *toastmasters*.

Ag Class

In the 1940's most of the farm boys took classes in high school called agriculture and the girls took homemaking classes. We had a remarkable Ag teacher by the name of Mr. Vrooman. We became members of the Edmeston chapter of the FFA (Future Farmers of America). The FFA was, and still is, a national club of future farmers.

As president, I was required to attend a county meeting one night in the nearby town of Laurens, NY. Mr. Vrooman drove our Vice President and myself to this meeting. After the meeting we started for home in a very dense fog. The farther we went the foggier it became. All we could see was the white line on the side of the road. Using it as a guide, we were moving along at about 5 to 10 MPH when the road suddenly took a very sharp right turn, becoming extremely bumpy as the white line disappeared. Mr. Vrooman asked us boys to get out of the car and look for the lines. We did and immediately started cracking up. Mr. Vrooman wanted to know what was so amusing. The white line that guided us to the sharp right turn was a railroad crossing line that he had followed, driving us down the railroad track.

Ag class started at 11:00 A.M. and ended at noon. The school cafeteria was opened at 11:00 for the grade school classes and the smell of food made us all hungry. Some of us boys would go to the cafeteria and buy an ice cream on a stick. We would then proceed to eat the ice cream while Mr. Vrooman was trying to teach us something about farming. He, too, was hungry and he made the announcement that this eating in class was going to have to stop. After all, he didn't have a chance to buy ice cream as much as he would like to. I immediately abandoned my chair, went to the cafeteria and purchased some ice cream on a stick (they cost a dime at that time). Returning to class, I gave the teacher his ice cream. He looked a little startled but he did thank me. Eating our ice cream became a daily ritual for a while. Finally he put a stop to it. Rumor had it that when he went home for lunch he wasn't eating as he should, so Lois, his wife, put a stop to our enjoyment. At times wives can be real annoying, even if they don't belong to you.

My First Car

In Ag class we had to raise an animal, or several, for an Ag project. My first animal was a registered purebred Holstein calf. I later raised two more calves (one died prematurely) and also 200 chickens that I later sold to my father. In the summer of 1948, I sold my best heifer to Stuart Rood (*my cousin with the mean father*) for $350.00. That was a small fortune in 1948. I took the money and made a down payment on my first car. A brand new 1948 Crosley.

After the war there were several companies that sprang up trying to break into the car market. Companies like Kaiser, Frazier, Tucker, Crosley etc., along with the many established car companies, now long gone out of business, such as DeSoto, Studebaker, Willis, Packard etc.

The Crosley was a four-cylinder small car. It wasn't a very good car. I had to pay $40.00 a month for two years, after paying the $350.00 down, as the car sold for about $1200.00. In the fall I realized that there wasn't any heater in the car, so sold my "*old friend*" the motor bike for $75.00, and bought a heater. Every time that I would get the car to go over 50 MPH, it would burn a valve and would cost me $25.00 to have them ground.

Car Payments

After the war a man named Tom Lockerbie built a six lane bowling alley behind the movie house and ice cream parlor. It had no automatic machinery. Two alleys had only a lever to press with the foot that brought up little pegs to set the pins on. Four of the alleys had racks to put the pins in, and you pushed an apparatus down, by its handle, to set them. We earned ten cents per game. On league nights (Mon. through Fri.) there were 60 games ($6.00). Thus I had a better and faster way of earning money than peddling papers. I set pins at least three nights a week and often in the afternoons (after school) and on Saturdays for open bowling. The bowling alleys were closed during the summer months, so it would seem to me that I could have had the summer off for fun in the sun.

The Best Laid Plans of Mice and Man — Go Down the Drain

My fun in the sun was short lived. My father had a way of finding me jobs. In the summer of 1947 when I was 15 years old, he found me a job driving a tractor for Emil Tophoven. Emil had a wire hay bailer and I was to drive the tractor pulling the hay bailer, while another kid hooked the wires that Emil would push through the slots from the other side of the bailer. As it turned out, hooking the wires would make a person's hands raw as you couldn't wear gloves, and the other kid and I finally had to take turns. One day I would drive the tractor and the next day I would hook the wires. We bailed hay all over that summer. We bailed hay in Edmeston, in New Berlin, in South New Berlin, in Gilbertsville, in Garratsville. We bailed hay for any farmer who could pay the price of ten cents per bail. What a hot, lousy job and I had been looking forward to a summer of fun, fun and more fun.

The first day that I went to work for Emil, we were haying on the hill behind his house. He was driving the tractor. The other kid and I were working the bailer. When it was time for lunch, Emil unhitched the tractor from the bailer and told me to drive the Case tractor down the hill to the house. I had never driven a Case tractor before. I started down the hill towards the house. The tractor began going downhill faster than it should so I applied the brakes. No brakes. Emil was shouting at me, but I couldn't hear him, and the tractor was gaining speed. I was headed towards the house and the kitchen where Mrs. Tophoven was preparing our meal. I had never met Mrs. Tophoven and I really wasn't ready to meet her this way. I knew that tractor was going to go through the house with me on it and come out the other side along with Mrs. Tophoven. I could just see the headline in the newspapers:

15 YEAR OLD HIRED MAN STEALS FARMER'S WIFE
BOTH WERE LAST SEEN LEAVING TOWN ON A CASE TRACTOR

SHE WAS RIDING ON THE HOOD SHOUTING: "DINNER IS READY"

OR THE EPITAPH ON MY TOMBSTONE:

What became of Grandpa Ray
He was hired to bail some hay.
He tried to drive an old Case tractor
But the brakes and clutch were another factor.
Down the hill that tractor sped
and Grandpa Ray lays here dead.

Since there was no stopping that tractor, I felt that there really wasn't any reason for both Mrs. Tophoven and myself to go to that big hay field in the sky, so I prepared to jump. In so doing, I took my foot off the brake. It wasn't doing any good anyhow. I later realized that the brake was a rod sticking up next to the seat, and that the pedal that I was so dearly ramming to the floor was the clutch. I was coasting down the hill. The tractor was in gear so, when I let up on what I thought was the brake, it suddenly let out an ear splitting whine and slowed so fast that my feet came up in the air and I almost went over the top of the hood. I hung on as Emil caught up with me, helped me to stop and shut off the tractor just as we neared the kitchen door. It could have been just another farm accident and tragedy, but for some reason God let me live that day. Maybe He wanted some more Fullers for the future.

Good Old Charley

The next summer, when I was 16, good old Dad came home with another job for me. This time it was on a farm south of the village for Charley Rathburn. Now Charley had been the hired man on this farm, for a number of years, when it was owned and operated by a man named Grover Hickling. One summer day when Grover was out in the hay field, a thunder storm had come up and he had headed for the house. There was a barbed wire fence across the field between him and the house. As he was crossing the fence, lightning struck it and killed him. This left Mrs. Hickling with a house full of kids and no man to run the farm. Needing a man and Charley being handy, she married him.

This all took place several years before I went to work for Charley, but Charley was still farming with the same outdated tools that were left to the widow Hickling. She just wouldn't buy any new farm implements. Grover did have an old John Deere tractor that was equipped with lug wheels instead of modern rubber tires. That was the only nearly modern piece of farm equipment on the farm. The tractor had no starter. To start it, one had to open petcocks on both sides of the engine to release the compression and advance the spark control located on the steering wheel. The next step was to turn the fly wheel on the left side of the tractor. After several turns of the fly wheel, if you were lucky, the engine would cough and finally start. You would then have to run around to the right side of the tractor and shut off the petcock to build up compression, then run back to the left side and shut off the petcock, then jump into the tractor seat, retard the spark and advance the accelerator to "rev" up the engine. If you were fast enough you could do all of that after just a few turns of the fly wheel, but usually the engine coughed out before you could get everything in place and the entire procedure had to begin all over again.

Charley thought it great fun watching me run around that tractor, and seldom would he come over and close the petcock on the opposite side of the tractor for me. Starting the tractor was a memorable affair, but driving it was something else. Charlie's farm was hills and rocks. The tractor had lug wheels and every rock or stone that met a lug would give you a bounce that would knock your teeth together, until you learned to keep your mouth wide open, or tightly shut and your tongue sucked in so as not to bite it.

My morning breakfast usually consisted of a cup of coffee and one of my mother's big molasses cookies. As long as I wasn't working very hard, this little breakfast held me just fine. The first day that I reported for work at Charley's place, I had eaten my cookie, drank my coffee, and mounted my motorbike and, as ordered, reported for work at 7:00 A.M. sharp. I leaned my motorbike on the barn, walked over to Charley and told him that I was ready to go to work. Charley said, "Not so fast, we haven't had breakfast yet." I told him that I had had a big cookie but he just laughed. Saying that no one was fit to work on a cookie and that we were going to be doing some real work, he ordered me to come into the house with him for breakfast.

Mrs. Rathburn seated me and handed me a enormous bowl of oatmeal and a banana. I cut the banana into the oatmeal, added some brown sugar and cream and ate it. I was now ready to go to work. Charley said, "Not so fast, we haven't eaten breakfast yet." I was trying to explain to him that I had, when out of the kitchen came Mrs. Rathburn with a big platter of fried potatoes, a platter of bacon and another platter of fried eggs. I looked around to see who else was having breakfast with us but didn't see anyone. I was hoping that, perhaps, they might be expecting company. I learned very quickly that I was the company. I was very abruptly educated to the fact that part of my job, on the Rathburn farm, was to eat breakfast with the Rathburns. These good people not only fed me a copious breakfast and dinner, but they also started my pay from the time I arrived at the farm until I left in the evening. It is the only time in my life that I can remember getting paid to eat and to eat someone else's food at that.

One night we had a light rain, so in the morning we had to wait until the hay cocks were dried out before we could start loading hay. While waiting, Charley and I cleaned the barn. We had the manure wagon completely full of real sloppy, summer-time cow manure. Charley told me to drive the load to the top of the hill on the other side of the road. I asked him where he was going to ride and he replied, in the wagon. I said that the manure would be up over his boot tops to which he retorted that that was not a problem. He simply pulled off his boots and socks, rolled up his pant legs, grabbed the manure fork and jumped into the manure wagon. The manure was well over his knees. I did the driving and he did the spreading. When we were finished, he asked me to drive down to the flat land by the creek and there he jumped out and went wading. Charley never complained about having any corns or blisters on his feet and I might just know the reason why.

We spent our days in the hay field in the hot sun, pitching hay by hand. Charley would pitch and gripe, pitch and gripe, pitch and gripe. All he ever talked about was his wife. How frustrating it was to live with that woman! She expected him to run the farm with worn out and out-dated equipment. She just wouldn't buy anything for the farm, but almost every year she would come home with a brand new Chevrolet car. Charley didn't have a car and she wouldn't let him drive her car. Every time he had to go to town for anything she would drive him. Many times she would go somewhere during the morning in her new car, but she would always get home in time to feed us a generous meal at noon time.

Charley, wanting some of the credit, would tell me how he helped raise "*that woman's*" children after Grover was killed, and how well they had turned out (and they had too). He said, "that woman" always took all the credit. Charley liked going to the Grange and said often "*that woman*" would go and leave him at home after he had done all the day's work. He complained that she would go here and there, and he was left at home with all of the hard work to do. He would go on and on everyday and I couldn't see, for the life of me, how he could stand it living with "*that woman.*"

One night it had rained very hard. The next morning, after breakfast, Charley announced that he and I were going to clean the barn, and that by the time we had finished, the hay cocks would be dry on top. He would spread the manure by himself. He advised Mrs. Rathburn that she could go with me down to the hay field and turn the hay cocks over, as they were soaked through and wouldn't dry on the bottom.

Sure enough, after we finished cleaning the barn he handed "*that woman*" a pitch fork and off we went down to the lower field to turn the hay cocks. We hadn't any more than gotten out of earshot when she started in on Old Charley. I was only 16 years old but I had to listen to her side of the story. She told me what a worthless man that Charley was. He was nothing more than a hired man until after her husband was killed. She married him, giving him a home, and he was allowed to run the farm pretty much as he liked, but he didn't seem to like to run it very well. "*That man*" always was after her to spend money on tools and equipment that he certainly didn't need. Her first husband, Grover, never complained about the tools being old and outdated. [She pointed out the spot on the fence where she had found Grover almost twenty years before]. I mentioned that maybe the tools were new when Grover was alive. She insisted that they were like new now, since Charley certainly hadn't worked hard enough to wear any of them out.

I became quite concerned, one day when I went to work, and poor Charley wasn't feeling quite up to snuff. I prayed that Charley wouldn't take real sick and die on me, as I was sure his widow would want to marry the hired man; and I was the hired man.

Note: Mrs. Rathburn is buried in the Union Cemetery in Edmeston with Grover on one side of her and Charley on the other. I am sure that there must have been some caring. I think that I was a sounding board for both of them at the time.

Do Not Try This At Home

That same fall, I was working for another farmer filling his silo, I was working inside of the silo. We were almost finished when a thunder storm came up. This silo didn't have a roof on it and I was at the very top. We had only one more load of corn to run through so we tried to beat the storm. I was pitching the chopped corn (ensilage) around the inside of the silo and was standing about five feet from the metal blower pipe. It hadn't started to rain yet, so the farmers were feeding the corn into the cutter and blower as fast as they could. I was pitching the ensilage as fast as I could. Suddenly I felt a yank on my arm and shoulder and heard a very loud **whack** that sounded very much like someone hitting the blower pipe with a baseball bat, trailed by a loud singing noise. This was all followed by an extremely loud clap of thunder and then silence, total and deafening silence.

The tractor that was powering the blower had shut down and no one was moving. Finally, I stepped to the side of the silo and shouted down, "what was that?" One farmer was rushing up the silo ladder and the other men were shouting, "Get down, get down we've been hit by lightening!" It didn't take long for me to get down. The men came over to me and a couple of them put their arms around my shoulders. They were so relieved that I was all right and some were visibly shaken. They thought that I had bought it.

What apparently happened was, the metal pipe pulled the lightning away from me. It followed the pipe to the blower, to the drive belt, to the tractor, that was powering the equipment, and stalled the tractor which apparently had grounded the lightning. Because I hadn't come over to the edge of the silo right away, they were all convinced that I had been hit. Only by the Grace of God, no one was touching any of the equipment as the lightning struck. A boy named Bobby Schraag had stayed home from school one day in 1943 to help his Dad fill their silo and he had been struck and killed by lightning. I had seen the place where Grover

Hickling had been hit and died. I knew that for some reason God had protected me that day. If He hadn't you wouldn't have a Grandpa Ray. Instead you would be reading my epitaph:

> *The day started out sunny and bright,*
> *By late afternoon it became dark as night.*
> *On top of the silo stood Grandpa Ray*
> *one more load and he could earn his pay.*
> *But the lightning struck*
> *and Grandpa was fried,*
> *but he finished his job before he died.*

The Cider Salesman

One Saturday in the fall of '48, Dick Rollins was with me in my Crosley station wagon and we ended up on Taylor Hill. Taylor Hill used to be a busy settlement years ago. In fact, the First Baptist Church of Edmeston was built on Taylor Hill. There was a school house and several homes, at one time, but all that remained was the eroded foundations and remnants of flower gardens and apple orchards. Even though the apple trees were several years old and not cared for in any way for years, they still bore fruit. Sure, the apples were full of worms. Apples always had worms. No one that we knew ever sprayed their fruit trees.

Well, Dick and I looked at all of those apples just going to waste and decided that maybe we should gather them up, take them to the cider mill and sell the cider. We loaded the Crosley wagon as full as possible and drove to the cider mill. We unloaded the apples, then went home and took some of my father's milk cans back to the cider mill to put the cider in after the apples were pressed. From there we went to the Ice Cream Parlor and Mrs. Forbes gave us several empty gallon jugs that Coke syrup had come in. We washed the jugs out, filled them with apple cider and set off down the road selling cider for fifty cents a gallon. As we sold all of our cider, the next Saturday we decided to do the same thing again.

We had a couple of big apple trees on the hill next to the chicken coups and my father said that we could have all the apples we wanted to pick. We picked them all. We had cider, cider and more cider. We had cider that we couldn't sell, but my father said that was all right as we could store it in the old wooden vinegar barrel in the cellar. We filled the 35 gallon barrel with cider and planned to come back and get it when we ran out. We never ran out.

My father said that we weren't to worry about the cider in the cellar as it would turn into vinegar and we needed vinegar. We soon forgot all about the cider. We didn't want to sell any more, as it was just too much work. We didn't work any more but the cider did. Before it becomes vinegar it ferments and becomes a very strong, spirituous drink that can give one a very happy feeling, followed by headaches and other, not so pleasant, after effects.

Several weeks passed and we had forgotten all about the cider business. One day my father disappeared. He was gone for three or four days and I had to feed and milk the cows, and clean the barn along with everything else. We knew that he had gone on a drinking binge but we didn't know where. No one had seen him downtown at the Gaskin House bar, nor could he be found at either the Eagle Inn, or the Green Top Inn located in the next town of New Berlin, where he was known to sometimes venture. One afternoon my mother heard a groaning noise in the cellar. She went down the stairs and there on the cellar floor lay my father. He was in dreadful misery and he was filthy. My mother got him upstairs, cleaned him up and put him to bed. The very next morning he was at the barn, very early, milking his cows as if nothing had happened. We had store bought vinegar that winter.

Applejack Mike

During the depression several of the farmers couldn't make it financially and so turned to other sources of income. We had a neighbor that lived down the road named Mike McManus. Mike had given up dairy farming and, for an income, had decided to make applejack.

Applejack is hard cider that is frozen in the barrel, when the spigot is opened, what comes out is almost pure alcohol. It is not far from, what is often called, white lightning. A pint of applejack was costly but it went a long way. Prohibition was at its peak and booze was supposed to be nonexistent. Applejack Mike was so busy that he couldn't keep up with his commitments. After prohibition was lifted everyone thought that Applejack Mike would go out of business, but he didn't. He was as busy as ever. Since his applejack was actually bootleg booze, he didn't pay the high taxes required on legal booze. His customers were loyal until the day he died, around 1938 or 1939.

It seems that everyone loved this old guy. My father often mentioned how much he missed old Applejack Mike.

Ice Fishing

On New Year's day 1949, I turned 17. The Sunday before New Year's day started out cold, but the sun came out and it warmed up above freezing in the early afternoon. One of my friends called and said that some of the guys were going to go ice fishing on Summit Lake. I had never been ice fishing before and it sounded like fun, so I gathered up my fishing gear, jumped into my Crosley and headed for Summit Lake. There were 5 of us that showed up and we all walked out on the ice, to the center of the lake, and chopped some holes to fish through. We hadn't been fishing very long when we started to notice that the water was gathering at our feet. It soon started getting deeper and deeper. Suddenly we heard a large "**crack**," and looking around saw that the ice had cracked all around us in a circle of about 35 feet and was giving way fast.

One of the boys, who was with us, knew the danger of drowning as he had lost one brother and his mother to drowning in two separate accidents. We were in the middle of the lake fully clothed and if that ice gave way we knew that we were gone. We looked at each other and, as if on cue, we each started for the shore in 5 different directions. Every step of the way we heard a crack, crack, crack, and the water was getting deeper and deeper above our feet. We each made it to our separate shores. We gathered together on shore and looked out onto a lake that possessed no ice whatsoever, only water. The ice on the spring-fed lake had completely broken up. I had been given another chance to become your Grandpa.

Let's Party

On New Year's night of 1949, Anna Claire Lockerbie was giving a party. Her father, Tom, owned the frozen food locker and the bowling alleys, along with some other businesses. There was to be an abundance of food. This was to be the genuine article, the social gathering of the privileged few, complete with a sit-down turkey dinner, party favors and games. The celebration of the year. Several of us high school celebrities were invited and we were supposed to bring a date if we had one. I had a girlfriend, Connie Sheldon, that lived near the village of Morris, but her parents wouldn't let her go to any party with those undomesticated kids from Edmeston. So I didn't have a date. We had heard rumors that a darling new blonde had migrated to our region, somewhere near Burlington Green on the road toward Garrattsville. What new girl wouldn't be flattered to be invited to a party, and by your Grandpa Ray at that. In the event that we couldn't locate her, we were prepared, to try to locate the McClean farm. The McClean's had a pretty blonde daughter, Margery, that I had an eye on, but had never really dated, because no one knew where she lived. It was difficult for attractive farm girls, living out on some back dirt road, to get dates when no one can find them. Not only that, she had some hefty brothers that were devoted to the family, and they weren't all that fond of *sissy* town kids, and I was considered a town kid. There were about 16 to18 kids in that family, and they took care of their own.

Red Benson, Dave Chesebrough, Gar Larson and I decided that maybe we should go over to Burlington Green, try to locate one of these girls and drag one of them back with us. Dave had his mother's new 1949 Plymouth. As we started up the hill out of West Burlington, Red said that he knew of a short cut over a dirt road that ran off to the left, at the top of the hill. So we took a left turn. Big mistake. The dirt road hadn't been plowed from the snow storm the night before, and the wind had blown a drift across the road approximately as high as the car. Dave said, "What do you think?" We all shouted "Go for it." The words had hardly left our mouths when we found ourselves on top of the snow drift.

A farmer named Sam Hill lived about a half mile up the road, and we were confident that he would lend us a couple of shovels to dig ourselves out with, if we could only get to Sam's place. None of us had boots or overshoes on, just street shoes or sneakers. We finally agreed that if Red and Dave walked the half mile or so and borrowed the shovels, then Gar and I would do the digging.

The car had stalled in the drift and Gar and I patiently waited for our friends to return so that we could warm ourselves up by digging out the car. They returned with two shovels and the good news that Sam had told them to leave the shovels standing in the drift after we were finished with them. It was evident that we were not going to get through the drift; just lucky if we could get off of it and back down to the main road. Gar and I shoveled for what seemed like an eternity, making little if any progress. It seemed like we had never seen so much snow. We were freezing cold. Red and Dave came out of the frigid car and took our shovels away from us. It was the only way to keep warm. We each took turns and spent the entire afternoon shoveling.

We finally dug our way off of that snowdrift, got the car started, backed out to the main road and directed the car towards home. We had just about enough time to go home, change out of those cold, wet clothes and go to the party. The other boys didn't have time to pick up their dates, so we all went without dates. The other boys' dates made it to the party on their own and even brought along a *lucky* spare young maiden that I immediately claimed as my date.

We had a Junior/Senior scavenger hunt one evening in the spring. Margery came to the village, to enjoy this affair, and she connected with me, as my partner for the hunt, but I never did find the McLean farm. My sources reported to me, that after high school, Margery married, moved to Long Island, and raised six kids. The mystery blonde that we were looking for, never made an appearance at Edmeston Central. We may have been chasing a false rumor, or she may have lived closer to Morris Central, and went to high school there. If the latter is true then it was her unfortunate loss.

FOUR

I do not give you the various episodes in their order of occurrence,

for they often overlapped and intertwined.

It has often been said that you are a product of your environment. My first 20 years were spent in the town of Edmeston. My father and grandfather were both products of Edmeston. My mother, Vera Welch Fuller came from West Edmeston.

Some people have said that my father married "up." The Fuller's were and had been small, *dirt poor* dairy farmers for generations. On the other hand, the Welch family were not only farmers, but they were cattle dealers and land speculators. Some in the Welch family became very wealthy

My mother had an Uncle named Ulysses Grant Welch who had worked his way through law school and became a well known and respected lawyer, district attorney and county judge. After he retired from his positions as judge, he continued his law practice in Edmeston.

The Judge

A little historical narrative

Grant Welch married into the Bootman family, one of the wealthiest families in the area. Mr. Truman Bootman, Uncle Grant's father-in-law, became the first Cashier for the *New* First National Bank of Edmeston in 1887. He rented two rooms in his dwelling for use by the bank. His annual salary was $500.00 a year. He received $60.00 a year in rent for the two rooms. In 1907 the rent was increased to $150.00 a year, including the heat. Later, a large two-story building was erected, almost across the street, on the corner of North St. and West St. The bank and Uncle Grant's law office, occupied the first floor of the building. New York Central Mutual Fire Insurance Company was on the second floor. Later a third story was added to the building for the expanding insurance company.

The insurance company had started on the second floor of the Old Opera House block in 1899. VanNess D. Robinson was elected Secretary and General Manager. VanNess Robinson was an exemplary businessman, highly regarded by everyone. I remember the sadness in the village of Edmeston in 1943, [near Thanksgiving], when VanNess died. His sons, Douglas and Ward, were able to continue building the business. I recall that, at the time of VanNess Robinson's death, there was only a handful of employees but by 1960 they had over three dozen employees. In 1960, Ward's son,

VanNess II and Doug's son, Theodore (Ted) were elected Assistant Secretaries. The company bought the Dorr Hickling farm, at the end of East Street, and built a new building. They later purchased the Guy Hickling farm, next to Dorr's and several other pieces of property. The company, today, is the pride of Edmeston with its sprawling offices, some satellite offices and over 1000 employees, many that commute to Edmeston from all over the area. The company is now known as *New York Central Mutual.* (www.nycm.com)

After World War II, Uncle Grant was getting on in age and so he took on a partner, a young lawyer just out of the army named Fred Loomis. It took Uncle Grant only a short time to get an appointment (to fill a vacancy) for Fred to become District Attorney for Otsego County. He later became a County Judge.

The Banister Ride

Shortly before we had moved to the village, the bank building had been enlarged. Uncle Grant had moved his offices to the second floor. Insurance offices occupied part of the second floor, and all of the third floor. A beautiful glass door was installed at the entrance way to the second and third floors. In the center of the stairs was a highly polished banister. I had never seen anything so beautiful and inviting. I had only seen something like this in the movies, where I had watched, fascinated, when someone had slid down the banister with merriment, landing proudly at the bottom.

I was now the paper boy for the village and I couldn't wait to get Uncle Grant's paper delivered. I ran up the stairs and dropped the paper at his secretary's desk. With the newspaper bag on my back, I mounted that beautiful banister. This was new and exciting. The only problem that I had, as a novice banister rider lacking any experience, was that as one slides down a polished banister the tendency is to pick up speed; and pick up speed I did. No one ever told me that banisters don't have any braking device and, once mounted, the banister rider is completely, totally and entirely on his own.

I have no idea how fast I was going in mph's as I flew down that beautiful banister. The banister stopped at the foot of the stairs but I didn't. The door at the bottom of the stairs had been propped open and I went through it going at a rather high rate of speed. I went flying out into the street landing squarely on my butt. I think that the people, in the law and insurance offices, thought that the world was coming to an end as I let out a rather loud yelp as I sailed through the door and onto the street. They all came running into the hallway and looked down to the bottom of the stairs. Out in the street, I was picking up my newspapers trying not to let on that my behind was hurting, and hurting real bad.

I gathered up my papers and did my best not to wobble, or limp, in front of all of those people. I finished my paper route and went home to take a closer look at my posterior. The way it hurt, I was sure that I had busted my butt. I looked in a mirror and was overjoyed to see that it wasn't busted. It was bruised and cracked but, at least, it wasn't busted.

Here Comes The Judge

I always felt somewhat intimidated by my Great Uncle U.G. Welch, as did many people, including my father, Clarence. As mentioned before, my father on occasion was known to tip the bottle a few too many times. On one of those occasions, he climbed into his car and, for reasons that only he knew or thought that he knew, he headed toward South Edmeston.

If for no other reason than to confuse my father, someone had put a curve in the road with a large tree standing where the road should have gone. When you are driving along, at a brisk rate of speed, and the fermented grape juice that you drank is now fermenting in your head, it isn't always easy to make quick decisions but my father could, and he did. He decided that the tree shouldn't be where it was and he tried to move it with his car. There was one issue, however. The tree absolutely refused to be moved and the car became totally redesigned. Even though he wasn't injured, he couldn't remember what it was that he had been driving or where he was driving to.

They hauled the car off in one direction and my father in another. When they finally dragged him into court, guess who the Judge was? You guessed right, none other than Judge Welch. My father once told me that, by the time they dragged him before the Judge, he was in perfect control of all of his faculties and, as the Judge was family, he was certain that he would be very understanding, scold him a little and send him home. Well, Uncle Grant did scold him and he did send him home, but without his license to drive. Uncle Grant made the declaration that, as long as he was alive, Clarence Fuller would never have a license to drive again. He did continue to drive, but he didn't get his license back until after Uncle Grant had passed away.

The Hitchhiker

Uncle Grant was never hesitant to let you know if you were doing something that he didn't approve of. This went for everyone. Being related, it seems that he had nothing better to do than to call my mother every time the paper was late, or if he had heard of some little thing that I might have done, or even thought about doing.

One Friday evening, I had gone to West Burlington to the skating rink with someone. I was about 14 years old at the time and, for some reason, I decided that I wanted to go back home. It was only 3 miles so I decided to walk, but, as I left the rink, I spotted Fred Loomis [Uncle Grant's law partner and the Otsego County District Attorney] driving toward Edmeston. I was of the assumption that he was returning from a hard day's work in Cooperstown, putting bad people away for life, and I put my hand up to stop him for a ride.

As it turned out, Uncle Grant was in the car with him. They had been in Cooperstown, but not on business. They had been fishing at Otsego Lake and were returning home. I climbed into the back seat of the car and Uncle Grant turned around and started a discourse on hitch-hiking; not just about the danger involved, but how could I lower the family standards and embarrass everyone in the family by becoming a common hitch-hiker.

The next day, he called my mother and gave her a lecture on raising young boys, even though he had never raised any children.

I knew that I was going to stay clear of this fellow, as much as possible. I didn't want any contact with him that could be avoided. This became a real concern of mine.

The D.A and The Girlie Show

I was 15 years old and the county fair was on in Morris, NY. I had a second cousin, by the name of Gordon Welch, who had joined the Navy at 17 and was home on his first leave. We were not close, as cousins go, but he wanted someone to hang around with at the fair so we went together. Gordon, proudly, wore his uniform and I, proudly, followed him around the fair grounds. We happened upon a girlie show. Out in front was a pretty little thing that was lacking for clothes, but not for looks, and as she danced on the little platform in front of the tent, the hawker was inviting everyone in for the greatest show ever for half a buck. Keep in mind this was 1947 when a buck was a buck. Gordy said, "Let's go in." I reminded him that I was only 15 and was afraid that I might get caught. He told me not to worry, that as long as I was with him and he was in uniform, no one would question us, so I agreed. He handed over a buck and we entered the tent. As we entered the tent, we were startled to see two New York State Troopers standing by the ticket taker eyeing me over very closely. I was sure that they would soon be putting me in handcuffs and taking me somewhere that I didn't want to go, but they just looked at Gordy and then looked at me, kind of eagle eyed, and asked me my age. I told them that I was 18. Gordy said to me, "I told you that you should have worn your uniform because you look so young." This seemed to satisfy the troopers as we were allowed to take our seat on one of the benches. Gordy wanted to be sure not to miss anything so we marched right up front.

As we continued to hear the music outside and the hawker telling everyone how the show was about to begin, I looked around the tent and who should be sitting three seats behind me, but Fred Loomis, the District Attorney with some of his friends. I was almost certain of two things. I was confident that he was there on official business, looking for juveniles that should be home and not in a girlie show tent. Secondly, I was positive that when he returned home, he would tell Uncle Grant that he had caught me in a girlie show, Uncle Grant would call my mother and my mother would put me in chains, for the rest of my life, just to keep me out of trouble.

It seemed like forever that the hawker went on and on, trying to fill the tent, before starting the show. All of the men were waiting, in great anticipation, expecting to see this pretty little thing come on stage and do whatever girls are supposed to do at girlie shows. I was sweating it out and looking cowardly over my shoulder at Fred Loomis, who would always look directly back at me.

Finally the show started. The music now was in the tent, instead of outdoors, and on stage came this fleshy woman that was, at least, 50 years old if she was a day. When you are 15, 50 is old. She danced around the stage trying to look sexy and as she started to remove her clothing the men began to boo. I'll say this for the old gal, she didn't let any of that stop her, she was unrelenting, perhaps because she saw no other career open to her. She kept right on with an air of self-assurance, determined that she was going to triumph. Off came everything except her bra and what they called a "G" string. This really brought on the boos and, with a movement almost bordering on grace, she unsnapped her bra and let it drop to the stage floor and everything else seemed to fall right along with it. The men were shouting to bring on the girls, but no young pretty girls ever came out. The pretty little thing outside was only a lure to get these love starved men to part with their money. The men weren't happy with the show and I could only think of one thing. How to get out of there.

I thought that the show would never end. Nervous and embarrassed, my stomach began to churn. I am not sure what made my stomach upset the most, Fred Loomis behind me or this outlandish looking woman taking off her clothes. It was probably a combination of both. The woman started doing some kind of gyrating with her hips and then her act became crude, vulgar and outright disgusting and I put my head between my knees and threw up. The men stopped booing and started laughing at me. The show finally ended. The hawker thanked everyone for coming, especially the kid with the splattered shoes, and everyone thought that was funny except me. I tried to slide past Fred Loomis, but he just gave a little nod of the head in recognition and turned and left. As I left the tent, the men were still laughing at the kid that tossed his cookies and Gordy Welch told me to get lost. I have not seen or heard from Gordy Welch, since that dreadful day over 50 years ago.

For several days after the fair, I waited for my mother to approach me regarding this ordeal but nothing happened. It took a lengthy period of time for me to realize that Fred Loomis was not in the tent on business. He was there for the same reason that I was, purely educational, an earnest study of the anatomy.

I now know that he was as worried that I would tell Grant Welch that I saw him at the girlie show, as I was that he would tell him about me. Also, I am now certain that he thought that I would tell everyone in town and that it would possibly get back to his wife. I don't know if it ever did get back to this wife or not, but I **did not** tell **everyone** in town. I did not tell my mother and I did not tell Grant Welch.

More Relatives

If you take the road out of Edmeston going east for a couple of miles then take a left turn onto a dirt road, about a half mile on the right is another dirt road going up a hill toward Taylor Hill. Some of the roads may be paved today and many changes have taken place, but in the 1930's and 1940's you would have found yourself passing the Glen Fuller farm, the Wilkinson farm onto the Nutt farm and eventually the Wakefield farm.

Glen Fuller was one of my father's cousins. His farm was well run. He had some modern equipment and a new truck, and even though his neighbors seemed to be hard up, Glen, appeared to be somewhat prosperous. Like most farms, the Glen Fuller farm had no indoor plumbing or electricity, but that didn't seem to bother cousin Glen. People said that the reason they had money was that they didn't waste any money on soap. Personal hygiene apparently was not important. We tried to pretend that they were not part of our clan, but everyone knew better so we were stuck with the facts. Glen, Jr. would never come to school unnoticed and it wasn't the fragrance of after shave. He had a younger sister, Margaret. I don't remember that she was odorous like her brother but the poor girl had to take the chiding that the Fuller family took.

The neighbors, the Wilkinsons and the Wakefields all had fairly large families. The Nutts were a smaller group. I don't recall exactly how the marriages went, but some of the Wakefields married into the Wilkinson family and/or vice versa. One of the Wilkinson girls married the Nutt boy. His name was Richard but everyone called him Boob. He served under General Patton during WWII. I think that Boob was the only boy in the family because I often heard that the old man had only one Nutt to carry on the family name.

These people were hardy and tough. How they eked out a living on those *scrub* farms is amazing, but they did and they did it **without** government handouts. They lived simply and worked hard. I always admired the resolve of these families. Hard times were just a way of life, not only for these families but pretty much for most of us farmers. Broke is broke. Poor is poor and we all felt it during these times.

Old Ben Wakefield and the boys had acquired an old John Deere tractor, with lug wheels, and they used it for everything including an occasional trip to town. They had constructed a small wooden box on the back of the tractor, so that the old man could ride in it. One day they had a terrible farm accident and the old man was run over by his own tractor. He was torn up miserably, so badly that his intestines were completely exposed along with some vital organs. The boys scooped old Ben up, placing him in the little box on the back of the tractor and headed for the doctor in town.

My parents witnessed the poor old man sitting in his little wooden box holding onto his intestines, as they passed by their house.

No one, including the town doctor, held out any hope for saving the old man. Somehow, they got him into an ambulance and took him to the Cooperstown Hospital where they cleaned him and sewed him up. After an extended stay, they sent him back home and he did live for four or five more years. These people were strong and hardy.

Somehow, a rumor got started around the village that the doctors couldn't get his intestines cleaned up enough to put back inside of him, so they replaced his intestines with those of a sheep. I never took any stock in that story, until it was confirmed that every spring they had to take the old man down to the barn and shear him.

The Ice Cream Man

A young man named Henry Miller used to get into the booze and drive his car around town like a lunatic. He finally married, moved to Richfield Springs and took a job on a farm. Soon having a bevy of kids, everyone believed that he had finally settled down. He may have, but he did enjoy an occasional visit to his favorite pub. One Saturday afternoon he went to town in Richfield Springs, which is on US Route 20. At that time there was no Thruway, so it was a busy road that passed through the center of the village. After Henry had purchased his groceries for the week, he made a slight detour, to his favorite watering hole for a couple of cool ones. He left sometime later, slightly out of kilter.

Getting into his car and starting down US Route 20 toward home, he noticed that the ice cream was melting all over the front seat of his car, so he rolled down the window and pitched it out. Just at that time, a New York State Trooper was passing in the opposite direction. The ice cream struck the trooper's windshield. It seems that the trooper took this as a personal indignity. He turned around and chased Henry and, according to the newspapers, the trooper charged Henry with a long list of infractions including assaulting a police car. Can you envision a man assaulting a police car. Some troopers just don't have a creditable sense of humor.

Edmeston Free Library

Every village needs a Free Library. Edmeston had, and still does have, a library. The librarian was an old maid by the name of Miss Gates. Miss Gates was nearly deaf and she had very loose, artificial teeth. Upon entering the library one could hear her counterfeit teeth continuously going click, click, click. When you went to the desk to sign out a book she usually didn't say anything, she would just stamp your card with the return due date, hand the book back and continue to click her teeth. On occasion, one might have a question. Miss Gates had a large horn shaped device, next to her desk, that looked somewhat like a cornucopia or, perhaps, it might have come off of my grandmother's old graphophone that we used to play music cylinders on. The device was called a hearing horn. If you wanted to speak to

Miss Gates, she would put the small end into her ear and you would shout into the wide part. You knew that you had made contact when her teeth would go from a click to a clatter. She would then shout back at you. She couldn't hear herself talk so people often got into friendly shouting matches with her. The day did come when she acquired a real hearing aid, but that didn't help control her loose upper plate.

On Sunday morning you could always find Miss Gates in the Baptist Church, third pew from the front, next to her friend, Miss Chesebrough. Always in the front pew was Ducky Jacobs. Ducky was slightly hampered with a simple-mind. She was probably about 50 years old and lived with her mother. She was short and you couldn't always see her sitting up front, but as people came into the church, or if there was a noise behind her of any kind, her head would pop up over the pew, turn about half way around, looking much like an owl, and then she would duck back down. That is how she became to be known as Ducky Jacobs. Church services were always interesting. Miss Gates would click her imitation teeth and Ducky's head would pop up, do a 180 degree turn then pop back down out of sight, until the next series of clicks.

The Baptist Church installed a young, new preacher who started preaching some pretty powerful stuff. Some people were pleased with the man and some were not. Even though

I was very young at the time, I knew that the preacher was getting into some very heavy stuff when Miss Gates would stop clicking her teeth and, after a period of silence, there would be a loud *klunk* instead of a click, Ducky's head would pop up about 10 inches over the pew, do her 180 degree turn and then disappear.

Out of High School

I graduated from high school in June of 1949 at the age of 17. The class consisted of 13 boys and 4 girls. The joke at the time was that, Edmeston being a farm town, the farmers all wanted boys to work the farms. If a girl was born, they threw her back.

I sold Fuller Brushes door to door for a three or four weeks after high school. I got my first real job in Norwich, NY for W. H. Dunn & Co. which at that time was the Victory Market Chain of grocery stores. The pay was $27.00 per week and the week was a 5 1/2 day week (45 hours), meaning that even on Saturday I had to drive the 25 miles each way to work the required half day. This breaks down to 60 cents per hour.

The Kraft Cheese factory in South Edmeston was hiring in 1949 but you had to be 18 to work there. The pay was $1.00 per hour. I met with the plant superintendent on New Year's

Day of 1950, my 18th birthday. He hired me and I started work the next afternoon on January 2, 1950.

Not All Work and No Play

I did try to enhance the work place at the Kraft Foods factory. Sometimes a little horse play was involved.

Working in a cheese factory, we had access to several water hoses and at times someone would get a wet surprise. Usually the target was never certain who did it for sure. Often the night foreman was the object of our attack. Our job was to clean the holding tanks, the separators and all of the stainless steel pipes had to come down and be washed and put back in place. Some times the pipes didn't get put back exactly as they should. A two inch pipe full of cold water, with an elbow aimed exactly where the foreman would sit on his little stool, could be the highlight of a night's work. By rigging the switch to the pump to a wall switch in another part of the factory and with the aid of a look out to signal when the time was right, the poor guy was never certain if the sky was falling or if the roof had sprung one enormous leak.

We all kind of picked on one of the men that we worked with. He was what you might call a "*hard nose*" and wasn't at all popular with the guys. One night I "*accidentally*" hit him real good with the cold water hose. I did this on the sly but, apparently he wasn't as dumb as I thought as, he quickly figured out who nailed him. Later that evening he actually tried to drown me.

I was often the one directed to clean the huge cheese tanks. After climbing inside one of them this man sneaked up and closed the hatch door, securing it from the outside. He put a cold water hose in through the pipe opening at the top, where it was impossible for me to reach, closed the drain opening at the bottom of the tank and turned on the water.

Fortunately, the foreman started to miss me after I had been gone for a long period of time and sent another worker to look for me. The workman climbed up the ladder of the tank and looked in the peep-hole. There I was swimming around inside an enclosed tank; clothes, boots and all with no way to escape. He shut off the water, opened the drain at the bottom and soon I was free. We all agreed that this man had intended to drown me in that tank and some of us pondered a way to get even. Both of us had almost been terminated over this incident so everyone knew that a water war was out of the question.

One Skunk Deserves Another

Finally an opportunity did present itself. A couple of us hard workers were doing a little "*goldbricking*" (relaxing on the job) out behind the factory when we surprised a skunk in an open cream bucket. One of the guys popped the lid on the bucket and put it (skunk and all) into the car of my adversary. The skunk was not delighted to be in this small confined space and on the drive home he made his presence known. The lid came off of the bucket and this animal was soon expressing his loathing for his situation with his tail in the air.

This man had moved to our area from New York City to become a farmer. Not knowing anything about farming, he soon realized that his cows weren't producing much milk. This required that he get a night job in the factory to support his family. No one ever told him that, to get a cow to produce milk, you have to generously feed them. This he didn't do.

He became totally frustrated with his animals and beat his cows using both fists. In fact, he was unable to come to work at the cheese factory because he had broken both of his wrists. The S.P.C.A somehow got wind of his mistreatment of his animals inspected his farm and discovered that the cows were nearly skin and bone. He hadn't been feeding the poor animals and so they had to be destroyed.

This is the kind of man that didn't like me. This is the kind of man that I didn't like. This is the kind of man that the skunk didn't like.

Romance

During the summer of 1949 I had time to do some dating. In high school I had become devotedly attached to a girl that lived in Morris, NY named Connie. I had a predicament. Whenever I made a date with Connie to go to the movies in Oneonta or anywhere else, I had to take her parents along. Now I really favored Connie but her parents didn't turn me on at all. I would sometimes let her father drive my Crosley, as that would give me a chance to sit in the back seat with Connie, but her mother would always keep watching us so that we couldn't do any kissing or "*such nonsense.*"

I had also met a girl, Irene Lamb, from Brookfield High School that I admired, but she actually lived on the other side of Brookfield in a community called Hubbardsville. We dated several times, mostly going to the movies, but it seemed like a long drive to Hubbardsville, which was all right in the summer, but in the winter I began to neglect her.

During the time that I was working in Norwich, a couple of girls, Virginia and Dorothy Whitmore from New Berlin, came to Edmeston to work for their Aunt Rachel Bagg. Rachel was involved with caring for some of the children from the Otsego School for Backward Children. She was a very good friend of Miss Chesebrough, the woman that owned and operated the school. David Chesebrough and I started dating these two girls almost every weekend. I dated

Dorothy and he dated Virginia. One night coming home after roller skating in Norwich, Dave suggested that we change girl friends as he said that he liked Dorothy better, and it was obvious to me that she liked him, so we traded. I think that he threw in an old baseball glove and a couple of candy bars in the deal. We were both happy with the arrangement as I liked Virginia a great deal more anyhow.

I soon discovered that my relationship with Virginia was rather unstable. Dave did eventually marry Dorothy so I guess that he made a good trade, but I couldn't seem to get real close to Ginney. I soon found out the reason why.

How I met your Great Uncle Frank

I soon encountered a rival. Virginia had been going very steady with a guy from New Berlin, a Nazarene minister's son, named Frank Chase. Dave and I had started going to New Berlin every Sunday to the Berean Baptist Church with Dorothy and Ginny. If I had met or even seen Frank there it hadn't registered in my mind. I think that I was more interested in girls at the time.

One delightful evening Dave and I had a date with these two girls to go to Chesebrough's cottage on Summit Lake. Their Aunt Rachel was gong to chaperone us and drive us to the lake in her brand new Packard automobile. We were all at Dave's house loading Rachel's car when into the driveway comes this ancient, time worn car with a youthful driver. Someone said, "It's Frank Chase." I said "Who is Frank Chase?" I soon learned that he was a boy from New Berlin that the girls knew and apparently knew real well. Rachel, immediately invited him to come with us on our little outing and, would you believe it, the confounded guy came along. I didn't realize that Frank had a thing going with Ginny until after we had finished eating.

Frank pointed out that it might be nice to go canoeing. The problem was the canoe wouldn't hold five people. Actually, it really wasn't large enough for four. But since Frank had made the suggestion, Dave invited him and the two girls to go. This left me at the camp with Rachel, our chaperone. To say the least, I wasn't happy being left behind and was almost elated when a motorboat came speeding by and the wake of the boat capsized the canoe and all four of its occupants were dumped into the middle of the lake. It never occurred to me that they could be in danger as Dave and I, and several of us boys, had not only swam across the small lake several times but had made the swim both ways (always accompanied by someone in a boat). Rachel couldn't understand how I could remain so calm. She was screaming, "they are in the water, they are in the water." I didn't know that Frank was recuperating from a broken leg and the girls weren't very good swimmers. Fortunately, the motorboat returned and fished them all out of the lake and deposited them on shore with apologies. Rachael drove us back to Edmeston, dropped us boys off at Dave's and took the girls home. Dave let Frank borrow dry clothes and we sent him packing.

How I Met Mary

The Mother of My Children

Summer ended and the girls went back home to school. They only returned to Edmeston weekends to work. Dave continued dating Dorothy through the fall. I did take Virginia roller skating a couple of times, but Virginia was also seeing Frank regularly as they were in the same school and had been going together before she ever came to Edmeston to work. I still had my girlfriend, Connie (and her Mom and Dad) in Morris, who I was seeing frequently, and was dating some other girls, but I was a thorn in Frank's side because I had an occasional date with Virginia.

One cold Friday night in January of 1950 after a special service held at the Berean Baptist Church, Frank, invited me to his home. It was the Nazarene Church parsonage, located upstairs over the church. He fried me a hamburger and some potatoes and we sat and talked as we ate.

I noticed a girl in the dinning room studying the Sear's Catalog and I asked him who that was. He said that it was his sister and not to pay any attention to her. She looked pleasing to me so I started a conversation with her. I judged that, perhaps, I might take a fancy to his sister. Frank said that he knew a girl that lived in Johnson City that I would positively like, and that we could drive down the next day and I could meet her. He was confident that I would fall in love with this girl and thus would leave Virginia alone. I spent the night at his place but our plans to go to Johnson City were altered. A bad snow storm had sneaked up on us during the night and we couldn't go anywhere. I had a chance to get very acquainted with his sister, Mary, during the day and we hit it off real good. In fact, I started making excuses to stop at Frank's place quite regularly, especially when I was almost certain that Frank wasn't there. That way I was able to see Mary.

On Christmas night (1950) I married Frank's sister, Mary, who had just turned 16 years old. On February 10th of the following year, your Great Uncle Frank married Carol Douglas, the girl in Johnson City that he was so certain that I would fall in love with.

Virginia has had to make her way through life without either one of us. *That is so sad.*

Another Close Call

or

This is about as dumb as it gets

On Wednesday, June 28, 1950 I was in an automobile accident. There was a rumor that Kraft Foods was going on strike. The Union wanted $1.15 an hour for the workers and Kraft was only offering $1.05. The dispute was finally settled for $1.10. In the meantime, Red Benson and I thought that maybe we should get a job in Richfield Springs, NY at the tannery. So about 9:00 o'clock we picked up Dick Rollins and headed for Richfield Springs.

Red was driving, Dick was on the passenger side and I was in the middle. We had some fire crackers and I would light them from the cigarette lighter and they would toss them out the window as we sped through the countryside. The difficulty came when I lit a fire cracker for Red and he tossed it out the window with his right hand while his left hand that was doing the steering followed the turn of his body and we went off the road. The car overturned several times. My head apparently hit the dashboard and I was knocked out cold. Red and Dick only had pieces of glass imbedded throughout their bodies and spent the afternoon in the hospital getting them removed.

Someone dragged me out of the car to the side of the road. I came around enough to hear a State Trooper say that it looked like this one wasn't going to make it. I guess that I looked critical. I came back to this world late in the afternoon. I was in the Cooperstown hospital. I had been out for several hours. My head was battered rather badly and I looked a fright. They did several X-rays on my head and brain but *"they couldn't find a thing"* so they kept me there until Friday and sent me home.

After I returned home, I went down to the garage to where they had towed the car. To this day, I don't know how any of us lived through that accident. The roof of the car was crushed down, almost, to the seat and every window had been shattered. Someone was looking out for your Grandpa that day, if they hadn't been you wouldn't have a Grandpa Ray.

And Life Goes On

After the wedding on Christmas night, 1950, we went to Niagara Falls but it was cold and everything was frozen so we returned in May of 1951 when it was beautiful.

We lived with my parents for a couple of months until we could find a place of our own. We then rented a small apartment over, what was then, the Post Office for $25.00 a month including heat and utilities.

I continued working at Kraft foods until early June of 1951. The Korean War (excuse me, conflict) was going full tilt and the military wanted men. I tried to convince the draft board that I was just a boy in men's clothing but they picked on me anyhow. I knew nothing about military life and didn't want to. But ...

Bon Voyage

FIVE

The *Misadventures* Of An Airman

In 1951 the Korean War was raging and the military needed men. The draft was in effect at that time and, because I was married, I had a 3A deferment. However, living in a farm community many young men of draft age had a farm deferment which counteracted other deferments including mine. In the spring of 1951, I received a notice from the draft board that I had been reclassified from 3A to 1A. The letter that accompanied the notice said that I was scheduled to be drafted at any time.

I have always skirted around any questions regarding my military service because the particulars were too involved to try to unravel all at one time. The details are too lengthy to attempt to explain in a few words.

Knowing very well that I didn't want to be drafted into the U. S. Army and probably end up in the infantry, I decided that it was best to enlist in the Air Force. I went to Utica and enlisted. The day that I was to report, I went to Utica, was put on a train with some other recruits and conveyed to

Syracuse where we were brought to the Air force Recruiting Office in the Chimes Building at 500 S. Salina St.

We were sworn in and later taken to dinner, then to the Hotel Syracuse to spend the night. Early the next morning after breakfast, we were assigned to a Greyhound Bus and taken to Geneva, NY. We were then boarded onto an Air Force Bus and driven to Sampson Air Force Base south of Geneva. Sampson AFB had been a Naval Training Base (Boot Camp) hurriedly built during World War II and it was closed shortly after the war. When the Korean war started, the Air Force reopened the base as a basic training facility. It was badly in need of repairs. The buildings were almost all constructed of wood, since the base was originally built to be a temporary base for the Navy. As we entered the main gates of the Air Base, I suddenly felt very lonesome. I realized that I had never been away from home before. The senior class trip to NYC, in April of 1949, had been with friends and anywhere else that I might have gone to was always with friends or family. I was terrified. We drove past the Headquarters Building, which was impressive, but beyond that there was nothing but barracks, drill halls and drill fields. What a depressing sight and I had no friends. We were dropped off in front of one of the two story barracks that had a sign that read, "3762 Training Squadron, Major G.L. Redd, Commander." We were ordered inside where we met our "DI" (drill instructor) a staff sergeant (they still called them sergeants then), and the rest of our group.

Even though the Air Force, which was the Army Air Corps during World War II, had officially become the Air Force in late 1947, it was still changing over from army uniforms and all army identification. So we were not to be called a Platoon, we were Air Force. We were to be called a Flight. We had 60 men (boys) in our Flight. The barracks were two stories, thus each building would hold 120 men. The only *partitions* were open cubicles with four double bunks to a cubicle. After being assigned a bunk, we were given an Air Force Hand Book and told to read and study it. We were marched to the mess hall, marched to a building where we received a $10.00 advance on our first month's pay. After being marched to a building and ordered to give a barber a dollar for a hair cut, our hair was shorn to the scalp. From there we went to the Quartermaster's Corps for uniforms. After we were measured, we acquired our olive-green fatigues that were really coverall's and a khaki dress uniform with a khaki dress cap. We were carefully measured for our shoes and military boots as we were going to march in those boots. The first and the second day kind of blended into one.

We were ordered to "hit the deck" at 4:30 AM, ordered to shave, shower etc., and be ready for roll call at 0500 in front of the barracks. We made it and from there were ordered to mess. We spent a couple of hours learning how to march and were then marched to the medical building where we were to receive our shots and our final physical along with our dog tags.

Sometimes Things Go Wrong

Our Flight got off to a very bad start with our Drill Instructor. We were instructed to line up single file and were led into a room that had Air Force Nurses, Doctors and Corpsmen on each side of us. They all had needles in their hands and plenty more where they came from. As we walked between the rows of nurses and medics, we received shot after shot in both arms for every disease ever known to man or beast. After we were finished with that, we were ordered to another room and a very thorough physical exam took place from hair to teeth to toes.

From there we were ordered into another long room where we were ordered to take off all our clothes and line up single file. An Air Force Captain, who was a doctor (proctologist) came in and ordered all of us 60, naked young men, to bend over and as he came to each of us we were to spread our cheeks with both hands as he gave us a close up examination.

As the doctor prepared to examine one of the recruits and stooped down for his "*close up*" the recruit spread his cheeks and broke wind into the doctors face. The noise was impressive but not as much so as the noise made when the doctor slapped the recruit across the rear end so hard that he went sprawling onto the floor face down. One recruit started to snicker. Right away all 60 of us were cracking up and we couldn't stop laughing. The Captain (doctor) ordered us to stand at attention, but most of us couldn't even stand up straight. He turned to our Sergeant and commanded him to order his men to stand at attention.

We finally made it to attention but someone snickered and we were all off laughing again. Now he had 60 naked recruits standing as near to attention as we could, while laughing our heads off and our sergeant screaming at us and the Captain (doctor) ordering him to get "his men under control." All of the fanfare soon brought in a Major and a Lt. Colonel who were probably doctors too. They conferred with the Captain and the three officers stood in front of us and made some promises to us that weren't very nice. Finally the laughter stopped. We all got ourselves under control. The sergeant took a real bad dressing down and the Lt. Colonel advised him that he was going to be put on report for not controlling his troops.

We now had one ticked off sergeant and he wasn't going to let us get away with that kind of performance. For punishment we had to "GI" the barracks. This meant that we had to scrub down everything, the walls, the bunks, the floor and the latrine. This took all evening after chow until lights out at 9:30 P.M.

The next morning at 4:30 we were again ordered to hit the deck, shave, shower, etc. and to be ready for roll call at 0500 in front of the barracks. I was 19 years old but I hadn't yet grown anything to shave so I skipped the shaving. Apparently there was some fuzz, because at inspection I caught a smell of the sergeant's breath when he put his nose close to mine and asked me if I had shaved. I explained that I didn't need to. That only made him real mean and nasty. I was ordered to dry shave but I hadn't even brought a razor with me, so he borrowed one from one of the recruits and I got my first morning shave. I didn't look any different, after scraping that dull, dry razor across my face a few times, than I did before. But I now knew who was boss. I was ordered to buy a razor at the PX (post exchange). I had learned to shave. I just hadn't learned how to grow whiskers yet.

Sometimes More Things Go Wrong

After mess the sergeant advised us that today was going to be the real beginning of our basic training. "The first thing that we are going to do is to learn how to march." We had already had some training regarding how to salute and who to salute on our first day but marching was more stumbling than it was marching He took us to the drill field. Sampson had several drill fields, as it was a basic training base, and the two biggest fields were about the size of 10 football fields so several Flights could train at the same time. We were lined up according to our height (15 in a line and 4 abreast). Being one of the shortest, I had the good luck of being in the very last row. We received a lecture on the different terms and were shown how to do a right face, a left face, about face, right and left flank, to the rear, column right and left, how to come to a halt with the proper count and how to do a skip to get back into step, if you found that you were out of step. We then set off marching down the field.

I was so glad that I was short because I had all of the other guys to follow and there was no way that I was going to mess this up after my chewing out at the morning inspection. We must have marched for nearly an hour doing our left and rights, learning to keep in step, doing column right and left and the right and left flanks. I was tagging right along superbly when suddenly the sergeant called, "To the rear march." I guess that some of the troops in the front row did hear the command and they did an about turn to the rear, but the rest of us didn't. We marched into our own men and several fell down on top of one another in the confusion. It was total chaos. I felt so superior that I wasn't one of those foolish looking troops getting up off the ground after several fell over each other. I was in the back row and was able to stop before the trouble started. We didn't hear the command because there were at least 15 other Flights training on the same field with sergeants calling out commands, but we were supposed to listen to only our sergeant.

After a proper dressing down we were off marching again. Again the sergeant called, "about face" and we all heard it this time. We did real good in turning around and going in the opposite direction. Bad predicament. I was now one of the leaders of the pack. I was in front and everyone was following and watching me, but I thought that I was doing very well. My left foot hit the ground as the sergeant called left and my right foot came down when he said right. I was really marching, left, right, left, right, hut, two, hut, three, hut, two—three—four. I noticed that the guys on either side of me weren't keeping up. I looked out of the corner of my eye to the right and no one was there. I looked out of the corner of my eye to the left and no one was there. These guys weren't keeping up like they should. I wondered why they didn't do the skip and catch up. Oh what the heck, that's their problem. Left, right, left, right, left, right, left, right. Where the heck are they? I peeked a little to my right. No one. I peeked to my left. No one. I turned my head around. No one. I turned around. No one.

There were flights all over the training field but none of them had my sergeant. I finally spotted my flight way down the other end of the drill field. He must have called another "to the rear, march" and I didn't hear him. He didn't seem to even miss me. If he hasn't missed me yet, maybe I can just run back down there and get back into formation without his knowing that I had messed up.

I went trotting down the drill field all by myself, a little concerned with what he might say if I were caught slipping into place. I passed a young man, who was a little older than I was, with a little gold bar on each of his shoulders. I had learned that this meant that he was a 2nd Lieutenant. Being a friendly sort of guy I thought it only proper to say hello. As I passed him I waved at him and said a big, "Hi." Instead of getting a big "Hi" back, I heard "**Airman Halt**." I halted. I turned around to see what might be the problem and he was in my face. His breath wasn't any better than the sergeant's had been, even though he was allowed to eat in the officer's mess. Must be they eat the same food, as they both had the same sour stomachs and nasty attitudes.

He ordered me to stand at attention in a rather high and girlish voice, and I stood at attention. He said, "Do You See These Gold Bars?" I answered in the affirmative. "Do You Know What They Represent?" I answered that I thought that they meant that he was a 2nd Lieutenant. He said "they mean that I am an officer of the United States Air Force and a leader. I am to be treated with the respect due an officer of the United States Air Force or any other military officer." He went on to inform me that it is required of every enlisted man or woman to salute any and all officers. I said that it sounded like a good idea to me and I gave him some kind of a salute and started to walk away toward my flight. I was afraid that my sergeant was going to miss me.

I had taken only about two steps when a piercing little voice shouted, "**Airman Halt**." I stopped and turned around and discovered that I was looking at one ticked off 2nd Lieutenant. He said, "Airman, you have not been dismissed. I have not returned your salute and you, never, walk away from an officer until you are dismissed." He started in with a string of words like I had never heard before. He must have learned them in officer's candidate school because we were never taught words like that in the school where I went. It really is too bad too, because almost all of the words that he used would have been easy to spell as there weren't over four letters in any one of them, and with such easy spelling I could have easily have passed my English regents.

It seemed kind of funny to me that a man could be so darn mad and yet he kept giving me Eskimo kisses. His nose was actually touching mine and physically touching a recruit is absolutely prohibited, even for drill sergeants and especially for officers. Another problem, my nose was smarting. I had been out in the hot sun and it was burned a little and this guy kept wanting to rub my nose with his. I thought that only sergeants got into your face, but this guy seemed to rather enjoy the face to face contact.

When the excitement of rubbing my nose with his nose wore off, he asked me where my flight was. I pointed it out to him at the other end of the field. He wanted to know why I wasn't with them. I said that I guessed that they just got lost or something and that I really didn't know why they couldn't keep up with me. The Lieutenant proceeded to march me down the field to my flight, screaming at me all of the way like a little woman. He went directly to the sergeant and asked him if I was one of his recruits. When the sergeant reluctantly admitted that I was, the Lieutenant started in on the sergeant. How come he hadn't missed one of his troops. Why didn't this man know enough to salute an officer. He advised the sergeant that we were both being put on report. I was informed that I was "*always*" to salute an officer and ordered to return to ranks. I turned around to return to ranks but I neglected to salute the Lieutenant. I was ordered back by the screaming, pimple-faced 2nd Lieutenant and instructed to say, "Yes Sir," and salute. He continued, "Airman when you see an officer…**you salute**…do you understand that?" "Yes sir." "Return to ranks…dismissed." I stood at attention, saluted, did an about face and returned to ranks. Badly shaken and very embarrassed, I knew that I was to salute officers and also knew that I was in real trouble with the sergeant. This was only the beginning.

We continued drilling and marching. I had begun to catch on pretty good, or so I thought. We were marched to the mess hall. Approaching the mess hall I spotted another officer with little silver birds on his shoulders and another 2nd Lieutenant. I knew from my Airmen's handbook that this man was a *Full Bird Colonel*, ranking just under a General. I knew too that he must be pretty darn important.

As we marched by, the sergeant gave an "eyes right" and also a snappy salute but none of the recruits seemed to notice this very important man. I did and I had just learned that when you see an officer you must salute, so salute I did. The Colonel didn't salute back. The Airman's Hand Book said that all officers would return your salute and upon doing so you would immediately drop your salute. You are **never** to drop your salute until the salute has been returned. The Colonel called for the Sergeant to "*halt your flight*." He did. The Colonel walked directly to the rear of the Flight and straight to me. I thought that he was going to return my salute and congratulate me on my being such a good Airman, the only one that knew enough to salute an officer. Instead he called his aide, the Lieutenant, over with his clipboard and said, "Get that man's name and serial number." I was still saluting and the stubborn old Colonel just wouldn't return my salute. He finally realized that my hand was going to be stuck to my hat until he returned my salute. He finally did give me a kind of hand to the head salute and then he turned beet red in the face. Now this Colonal must have gone to the same school as the Lieutenant that I had encountered earlier, because he knew those same short words that were never over four letters, and he was even better at using them that the Lieutenant was.

I thought that he was having some kind of religious experience. He had more religious words in his vocabulary than a Baptist preacher and somewhere mixed in there was **"Airman, you never salute when you are in ranks."**

I said, "I didn't know that."

That is when he called the Sergeant over and ripped into him for not teaching his recruits proper military etiquette. He told his aide to get this Sergeant's name and serial number and advised us that we both were being put on report. I didn't know what all this meant but the Sergeant seemed to know. I thought that being put on report might be something like being sent to the principal's office. I found out later that the two do not compare. Being put on report is a very serious matter in the military.

After we were dismissed by the Colonel, we had one ticked-off Sergeant and I was really in trouble. I received a real chewing out from the sergeant, there was no way that I could eat any food as I was totally upset, and no one in the Flight wanted to sit near me or speak to me. The afternoon was spent drilling and after evening mess (I was too upset to eat anything) we returned to our barracks for additional instructions, followed by an order to "GI" the barracks because, "We have one recruit that was a real screw-up and the entire flight was going to suffer." It's the military way of getting at someone that they can't touch physically. If you get everyone mad at one guy, chances are that he is either going to shape up or ship out. I was ordered to "GI" the latrines by myself which was no small order. Their were 20 urinals, 20 toilets and 20 wash basins, each begging to be washed, dried and made to shine like new. Following that, I was to take the first 2 hours of guard duty.

It is required that a guard be posted by the entrance to the barracks at all times, 24 hours a day. During the day the barracks were usually guarded by what they called a floater, a person waiting for orders to be reassigned and nothing better to do. At night we were to take turns and we were assigned 2 hour shifts. After your shift, you were to wake up your replacement. You were then released from your duty and you could get some sleep. This night I was assigned to do double (2 hr.) duty for screwing up. This meant that out of a possible seven hours of sleep, I could expect three at the most. The next two days were horrible. No one would talk to me. I was doing double guard duty each night. The sergeant announced to the Flight, that because of me we were all restricted to barracks on Sunday afternoon. Normally, recruits got three or four hours free time to go to the PX, or to walk down by the lake to enjoy the scenery on Sunday afternoons. I kind of felt as if I was disrupting the entire United States Air Force and destroying the sergeant's career.

After doing double guard duty for three nights in a row, I couldn't eat anything as much as I tried. I was weak, tired, homesick and very depressed. I was wearing away fast. We drilled all morning and we had gone a long way from the regular drill field as we were now allowed to march on the roadways like seasoned recruits. When it came chow time, we had to double time it back to the mess hall.

It was a hot June day and when we arrived at the mess hall we were late and had missed our assigned place in line. The sergeant went inside to get us reassigned to another time slot and left us standing at parade rest in the hot sun with those hot fatigues on.

When the sergeant came back out of the mess hall, one of his recruits was napping on the ground at the rear of the flight. It was me. I had passed out, stone cold. From somewhere, two corpsmen came to my rescue. They stuck some smelling salts up my nose, gave me some water and got me back on my feet and back into line. I was okay now. Again we had missed our time slot and another flight had taken our place at mess. After some maneuvering the sergeant finally got us into the mess hall. By now I was famished and ready to eat. I was doing a great job of eating, but had really only started when the sergeant ordered us to "fall in." We were scheduled to spend the afternoon taking some kind of tests but because we were late we only finished part of them. This did not go well with our sergeant.

After the evening mess and some additional instructions back at the barracks, the sergeant proclaimed that we had a certain recruit that had generated some serious problems for him today. However, we were not going to have to "GI" the barracks. He said that he knew how to shape up a recruit in a hurry. It was something called the "*Wind Mill*" and that Airman Fuller was going to go through it.

I had had experience with the wind mill in high school. Our gym teacher had used it quite frequently. It involves everyone lining up in single file, except the recipient, and they are to spread their legs. The recipient is to get on his hands and knees and go between the row of spread legs as fast as he can. As the recipient passes through, each man is to take a powerful smack on his rear end with both hands.

In high school if the gym teacher felt that you hadn't smacked the guy hard enough then you were the next one to go through. I never could make myself hurt anyone and so I had been forced to go through the mill quite a few times but with only about 25 or 30 high school kids. I was able to handle that. Now I was looking at close to 60 young men that were ticked-off at me and they wanted blood. My blood. In high school no one really wanted to hurt anyone as we were all friends. This was an entirely different situation. I saw a long line of angry recruits just itching to do damage to me. I knew that they were going to love every minute of it and I had no assurance that I wouldn't have to go through it the second time.

I made a decision that probably changed my life for ever.

Enough was enough. I was doing as good as I was capable of. Actually better than many. I was keeping up with these guys and many of them had messed up too. I knew that the sergeant was frustrated at having been put on report, and a couple of times it may have been my fault. He felt that he needed someone to make an example of and I was it. No way was I going to take this crap. I had had enough. I had always been a bit of a scrapper. When you are small and skinny, you have to learn how to fight fast and you learn how to fight dirty. I said to myself, "Okay, Sergeant, if you want a show then you shall have one."

When he ordered, "Go," I went to my hands and knees. I scrambled past the first three guys receiving hard slaps on my behind and I still had about another 55 men to go.

The fourth guy received the surprise of his life. I came up on him with my head neatly placed where it would hurt him the most. I know that I took out at least one more guy, maybe two more before the brawl broke out.

There were fists and feet flying all over the place and a good many of them belonged to your Grandpa Ray..

When I regained consciousness, I realized that I was in the back of an ambulance headed for the base hospital about 5 miles up the road. With me were two corpsman and two Air Police. I also realized that I was in a white straight jacket. I also realized that I hurt. I drifted in and out of consciousness on the way to the hospital and remember struggling with the straight jacket. When I was ordered to calm down I recall that I cracked a little joke. I said, to the corpsman, "When I get out of this thing, will I be able to play the piano?" He replied, "Oh yes, you'll have no problem playing the piano." I said, "Oh good, I've always wanted to be able to play the piano." I remember them laughing but then I faded out again, I can recall nothing more until the next morning when I woke up in a hospital ward, held down to the bed with leather restraints. Two corpsmen and two doctors were looking down at me. One was a medical doctor and I later learned that the other one was a psychiatrist. I was in the *Psycho Ward*. This would be my home for the next 90 days. I weighed in at 93 lbs., my right eye was swollen shut and I hurt all over.

The Hospital

Nothing was broken. I had some bruises, including the real dandy on the side of my head that had probably knocked me out. I couldn't understand why I was in the psycho ward and not in the guardhouse (military jail), until about three or four days later when the psychiatrist called me into his office and read the sergeant's report to me.

The sergeant never mentioned the mill. He wrote that Airman Private Raymond Fuller had recently been showing evidence of severe mental anguish and depression. The report went on that Airman Fuller had gone berserk in the barracks and had attacked several fellow recruits and that he needed to be restrained in a straight jacket. He continued, that it had required several air policemen and corpsmen to subdue him. [I knew better, it only took a kick in the head to subdue me]. The report continued on about the sergeant's observation of the deterioration of my mental condition, compounded by stress and extreme nervousness and an inability to understand commands, and so on and so forth.

After reading the report, the doctor asked me if the statements were accurate and if I wanted to add anything to it. Hey, the hospital sure looked a lot better to me than the Air Force Guardhouse so I agreed 100% with the report. The doctor asked me if I remembered anything about the incident at the barracks and I told him that I did not. Actually, I don't remember a thing after the brawl started and why bring up the reason for the brawl? Let a sleeping dog lie. The sergeant had covered his butt and we were rid of each other and I was in the crazy ward.

The days in the hospital became routine. The ward held 80 men and we came from all walks of life and each had his own problems. We had all kinds of charlatans fabricating ways to get out of the service. One guy would go around all day talking to himself. He was real good at it too. We tried to trip him up but he stuck to it everyday, day in and day out and even into the evening. He never talked to any one of us, just to his imaginary friend. One guy was supposed to be some kind of a guru and would have a religious experience, from time to time, dropping to his knees and praying no matter where he was or who he was with. Even when we were marching (yes, we marched even while we were in the hospital), he would suddenly go down on his knees and pray and letting the rest of us stumble over him. His best prayer services came when the doctors came around. One guy claimed that he had no bowel control and made a point of eliminating himself especially in front of the doctors' offices, almost on a daily basis. He was discharged real fast.

The hospital mess hall was what was termed as an open mess, meaning that we could go and eat at anytime that the mess hall was open. Several of us would go to mess at a time and we would meet other Airmen and joke around. We would inquire which ward they were in, etc. When they asked me which ward I was in, I told them that I was in the *Fruit and Nut Ward*, because we had the fruits and the rest of us were nuts. This became a standard joke and the title stuck. We called it the *Fruit and Nut Ward* because placed next to the corpsman's station and by the doctors' offices were a group of homosexuals. We didn't call them gay in those days. We called them queer, or fruits, and often they were called pansies. Thus we had our fruits, the rest of us were supposed to be nuts. We called the area where the homosexuals were, "The flower garden."

One of the guys from the flower garden was a world champion baton twirler and dancer, and had appeared in several movies. I don't remember his name, but he was well known and could dance and twirl his baton better than any one that I have ever seen. He would put on a show for us just outside the ward on the lawn, with Seneca Lake in the background. It was indeed a real professional show. He had photos and film clips of some of the movies he had been in including a picture of Liz Taylor, (Liz was 19 at the time), kissing him, as well as some other famous actresses. We remarked how lucky he was to have all of these beautiful women around him but he said that he would prefer beautiful men. Most of us didn't understand what he was talking about, because homosexuality was a thing that was hidden in the closet in the 1950's. We knew absolutely nothing about it. They all offered to teach us.

Because we were not physically ill, we were able to continue with our basic training on a limited basis while in the hospital. After morning chow, since we were ambulatory, most of us from our ward would spend the morning drilling. We would march around the hospital. This took up a great deal of the morning, as the main corridor of the hospital was a mile long with four ramps extending down from the west side with six to ten wards off each ramp. The march around the hospital, we were told, was about four miles total, so we all would eat a big noon chow. However, in the 90 days that I spent in the hospital, I never weighed over 98 lbs.

Incidentally, it was a pretty well known fact that during this time at military mess halls (especially in boot camps and hospitals), a substance was added to the food called Saltpeter. Saltpeter is a colorless powder that has a cool salty taste and it was supposed to reduce the male sexual vigor. At the time, it didn't seem to have much effect, but I have come to realize that, possibly to avoid detection, perhaps only a small amount was added to the mashed potatoes at a time and the body didn't respond right away. I will have to admit though, that in the past couple of years I have noticed that the stuff has really started to kick in. It's finally working!

I had very few contacts with the psychiatrist and never once did he mention what had happened at the barracks. I never knew why they kept me for 90 days. The doctor said that it was a requirement. I thought that, perhaps, they didn't want to send me back to the Squadron until my unit had graduated from basic training and moved on. Finally, toward the end of my 90 day stay, the doctor reported to me that he was recommending me for a medical (honorable) discharge and that I would be sent back to base to wait for the papers.

Back At The Base

I was bused back to the squadron headquarters and reported to the O.D. (officer of the day). I was advised that I would be used as a runner and would do guard duty. As a runner I would take messages including the orders for the day from base headquarters, and deliver them to the various squadrons. Guard duty was very boring and it also assisted me in acquiring more trouble. Big trouble.

I would spend the mornings working as a runner. In the afternoon I would be posted at the barracks for guard duty. Guarding an empty barracks just isn't the most exciting job in the world. One starts to think about home and apple pie, and whatever else that might cross your mind. One afternoon the recruits had returned to the barracks and I was biding my time waiting to be relieved of duty. I was slothfully leaning against the wall when who should walk in but a 2nd Lieutenant. The same one that gave me all the flack back in early June. We immediately recognized each other. This man, to me was the most repugnant person that I had ever met and he identified my revulsion for him immediately.

When one is on guard duty and an officer comes into the barracks, the guard is supposed to snap to attention and call the barracks to attention. The recruits are to stand at attention at the foot of their bunks until the officer gives the order "to stand at ease, or, as you were." I did everything right except for one thing. I neglected to snap to attention. I just wasn't thinking of God and country at that moment. I had been daydreaming of home when the Lieutenant approached and it took a second or two for me to respond and to snap to attention. I had continued to stand at ease, looking at the little creep of a Lieutenant and spewing out revulsion with my eyes when he screeched, "Airman attention."

At that point he cut loose on me. They call it a "*dressing down*." I stood at attention and he again lodged his nose precisely on my nose and went into a four letter word tirade. I had never seen or heard of such a foul mouth officer. I have never seen any other officer ever get into a recruit's face. That was a specialty of the sergeants and, even then, there was never any physical contact. An officer is supposed to have more dignity than to scream into a recruit's face. There was no question about it, this guy belonged in our flower garden. He screamed like a little girl and acted and sounded just like the pansies that we had in the psycho ward.

I apologized with a, "sorry sir" and "it won't happen again, sir." That should have ended it but he wasn't going to back off. His voice became a shrill shriek and I knew that he was loosing his self control. So was I. My distaste for him was obvious and he demanded respect which I just couldn't give him. He became determined to completely humiliate and degrade me. He continued on and on in front of the new recruits. I could not tolerate any more of his insolence and I blew my stack and lost control of all common sense. I have been known to loose my "cool" on occasions and this, unfortunately, was one of those occasions.

I took one step back to get him out of my face. I admit that I was very surly and nasty, and probably spoke much louder than necessary as I said, "Sir, the way you keep rubbing our noses together, I know that you really want to kiss me so let's just kiss and get this thing over with. Or even better yet, you can take off those little gold bars that are supposed to make you a real man and let's meet in a more private place, and we can see what kind of a man you really are."

I, to this day, don't know what I was thinking of talking to an officer that way, even if he was a poor excuse for an officer. The fact is, he was an officer and I was a private. Even worse, I was only a buck private. I guess that I wasn't thinking or maybe I figured, what the heck, I had taken on almost 60 recruits, why not a 2nd Lieutenant and a sissy, petite, little one at that.

There was some muffled snickers from the recruits in the barracks that were still standing at attention, waiting to be ordered, "at ease." They never received that order. The Lieutenant became enraged and started ranting at both me and the recruits about respect for his little gold bars and the fact that "He Was An Officer." He was going to teach us to respect our superiors as we were mere nothings. He turned and stormed out of the barracks. The bewildered sergeant gave the order to the stunned troops, "as you were." He sent me packing. I kind of had a feeling that he didn't want to be a colleague of mine.

If You Dance, You Have to Pay The Fiddler

The next morning, I reported to the orderly room at squadron headquarters as usual and the OD (Officer of the Day) asked me to have a seat. He made a brief phone call. Shortly after he hung up the receiver, two Air Policemen came in and ordered me into their car. They drove me to the Headquarters Building and escorted me into a room where two well dressed men in civilian suits were sitting behind their desks and next to them was Major G.L. Redd. The two men introduced themselves to me and said that they were from the CIA (Central Intelligence Agency). The men explained the function of the CIA to me and told me that the CIA was established in 1947 and that it was kind of like the FBI of the military. They explained that the CIA had replaced the OSS (Office of Strategic Command) after World War II to conduct intelligence operations and to investigate internal military affairs. [Today, the CIA appears to be more of a spying agency, but they were in their infancy at the time and probably had very little else to do].

These men proceeded to tell me that I had been accused of (but not charged with) soliciting a homosexual act and to make matters even worse, with an officer of the United States Air Force. They were quick to add that this could be ruled as a criminal act subject to court-martial, that it was their job to investigate the matter thoroughly and that they would decide what, if any charges would be made. They had a statement, made by the Lieutenant, stating that I had asked for certain favors of him, including a kiss, and also that I had asked to meet him in a private place for what he expressed as "obvious sexual reasons."

Wow, I didn't just put my foot in my mouth, I almost put both feet in the guardhouse. I spent most of the morning in the "*hot seat*" being questioned by first one man and then the other. They described some homosexual acts to me, that I just couldn't believe could happen, and was asked if I had ever participated in anything like that. I was absolutely shocked at some of the things that they claimed men do to other men and they seemed to accept the fact that my dismay was genuine.

I was allowed to tell my side of the incident in full and explain that yes, I had offered to meet the Lieutenant in a private location but for fisticuffs and not a tryst. The CIA men concurred that the Lieutenant and I had some real bad chemistry between us and love was not in the offering.

The Major remarked that there was probable cause to hold me for battery against the Lieutenant. I explained that I was standing at attention during the time that the Lieutenant was chewing me out, that it was impossible for me to make any direct threat by touching his clothes or his body, and that the only touching that had been done between the two of us was his nose pressed against mine (witnessed by about 60 recruits and a sergeant). I said that this man was supposed to be an officer and a gentleman but that he was neither. The CIA men concurred that I had not committed battery against the Lieutenant and, most definitely, was not interested sexually in him. They suggested to the Major that it might actually be the other way around.

The CIA men had interviewed the Lieutenant earlier that morning, taking a statement directly from him, and it seemed to me that they were of the same opinion of the Lieutenant that I was. The Major was furious. He made no attempt to hide his contempt for me. I had stood up to one of his officers and no charges were going to be made by the CIA against me. The major insisted that I should be charged with something. The CIA men refused to charge me with anything. They reminded the Major that I had been in the psychiatric ward for 90 days. I corrected them by telling them that I had been in the Fruit and Nut Ward for 90 days. They asked me to explain what I meant by that and when I told them they both thought that that was hilarious. The Major thought that we were all **nuts**.

You can imagine what it was like for me. A 19 year old buck private recruit being brought before two CIA men and a Major and being questioned for over three hours with the threat of a court-martial and military prison. I was driven back to the barracks by the Air Police.

The Major and The Private

The next morning was a Friday. I reported to the orderly room for my assignment and was told to report to the Major. I knocked at his door, entered at his command, saluted and reported as ordered. He ordered me at ease and in a very fatherly tone, asked me if I would like to have a four day leave and go home. I told him that I expected my discharge any day and that a leave would probably be counter-productive at this point. He insisted that I leave that day. I advised him that I had no way to get home and he suggested that I hitch-hike. I had never done that in my life but he insisted. I advised him that I had been issued a khaki uniform and reminded him that the Air Force now required blue uniforms to go off base. He said that khakis were still okay as long as I had a dress blue cap. My hat was khaki. He called a corporal in from the orderly room and instructed him to get a blue cap for this Airman. In a very short time, I had a blue cap and a four day pass requiring me to return by midnight Monday. He even had the corporal escort me to the base bus that would take me to Geneva, where I could start hitching a ride down route US 20 toward Bridgewater and on to Edmeston. I had come to the conclusion that the Major had had a major change of heart and had decided that maybe he should do something nice for me. I had concluded wrong.

I did hitch-hike home. On Sunday afternoon I received a phone call from Sampson Air Base that my discharge was waiting for me and that I was to report to the base no later than midnight Sunday night. I made several calls and finally made contact with Jim Newton, a farmer that I had gone to school with, and Jim agreed to drive me back to Sampson, for a price, as soon as he finished milking his cows. He picked me up and we drove, as fast as possible, to Sampson Air Base. It was 12:10 when I signed in at the main gate.

I reported to the orderly room the next morning and was ordered to see the Major. The Major advised me that I had been AWOL (absent without leave) from 12:00 midnight to 12:10. He also advised me that he had sent my discharge papers back as I was not on base to receive them.

I knew then that I had been set up and I let him know that I knew it. He insisted that I return to basic training. He had the papers ready for me to sign. They were a waiver of my discharge. I said "There is no way that I am going back to basic training. My wife is due on October 12th and I expect to be there. I have a discharge somewhere around here and I expect to receive it immediately, as there is absolutely no way that you could have returned any papers since midnight." He offered me a little smirk and said that if I didn't do as he said, sign these papers and go back to basic training, he would issue me an Undesirable Discharge.

The Major displayed a copy of the statement that the 2nd Lieutenant had made and told me that the statement, along with my being AWOL (for 10 minutes) and the fact that he had ordered me back to basic training and I had refused, would be grounds for charging me with insubordination. Thus he had grounds to issue an Undesirable Discharge.

Well, again, I lost my control. I said, "Major, if anyone is insubordinate here it is you. You have my honorable discharge somewhere here in this office and you refuse to issue it. I know that the medical (honorable) discharge was here Friday, when you sent me off base with a four day pass, then you called me late Sunday afternoon to return by midnight. You knew that I had no transportation to get back by midnight. I made it within ten minutes; your charge of AWOL is phony and would never stand up to a court-marshal. I am going home and you can do as you please with your ridiculous little Lieutenant's phony statement, your phony AWOL charge and your phony charge of insubordination."

The Major was a big man. He had a big round face. He now had a big **red**, round face. A private never argues with a Major. I think that the Major thought that this private had gone crazy. He dismissed me and advised me to keep out of his sight until he sent for me. Three days later on October 12th, the very day that Mary was scheduled to deliver, I was ordered to report to the Major. I reported as ordered and the Major handed me an Undesirable Discharge, signed by him. He ordered the corporal to escort me to the base bus that would take me to Geneva, NY where I could catch a Greyhound Bus to Bridgewater, NY. I was allowed to phone home to have someone meet me and I was gone. My military days were behind me. I arrived home late in the evening and on the morning of October 13, 1951, Ray, Jr. was born.

No one ever advised me that I could have my discharge reviewed, possibly upgraded, if I could prove that I had been lied to and set up. I carried that monkey on my back for 25 years before I read in the newspaper that someone had had his discharge upgraded. I felt that I had nothing to lose so I wrote to the VA. I was informed by them that a person has 3 years after discharge to appeal, however, they would forward my request for a review to the Pentagon. Sometime later, I received a letter from Randolph Air Force Base in Texas that there was some irregularities in my discharge records. I had never officially been discharged according to their records.

My next thought was, Oh boy, am I in trouble now. Over 25 years AWOL.

Later, I received another letter advising me that my records were being forwarded to the Discharge Review Board, that there was an apparent error in justice and that an Honorable Discharge had been ordered but had never been issued. This letter also mentioned that there was no record of my being discharged. The letter went on to say that they were going to review my case at Randolph Air Force Base and that, in my absence, I would be represented by the American Red Cross.

About a month or two later, I received my Honorable Discharge in the mail along with some papers to fill out regarding mustering out of the service. I had never been mustered out of the military. I filled out the papers, returned them and in about three weeks I received a check for a little over $225.00. It was my mustering out pay from 1951.

An accompanying letter stated that I now was officially discharged.

I wrote to both the Pentagon and to Randolph Air Force Base suggesting that since I really hadn't been officially discharged in 1951, perhaps I just might be eligible for retirement pay. After all, I really was still considered an Airman for all of those 25 years.

They both ignored my letter.

SIX

Is There Life After Children

We brought Ray, Jr. home from the hospital after paying the $50.00 for the hospital and doctor. I went back to work at Kraft Foods on the night shift and I stayed there until the spring, when I became wearied of factory work. Freezers were coming into vogue, especially at farm homes, so I bought a panel truck and started peddling ice cream, in half gallon containers, door to door to farmers.

Many of the Chase family had moved to Ithaca. While we were visiting them, they suggested that we, too, might move to Ithaca. I would need to find a job. In checking out a bakery that hauled baked goods to Sampson Air Base, they suggested that, since I had a panel truck, I could build up a retail business on the base. The sales manager from the bakery and myself went to Sampson Air Force Base and snooped around. We found that all of the Squadron Headquarters had a squad room where coffee and donuts were available in the morning. I acquired a vender's permit, a badge and a number. I pinned the badge to my shirt and we went about prospecting. We landed some promises so we ordered out some bakery products. I was in business.

We stayed with Mary's, Uncle Dick, while I worked on building the retail business. I would arrive at the base about 6:00 A.M. Usually, a free box of doughnuts or sweet buns would induce a quick inspection and then I could go and sell my products. I was usually finished before 9:00 A.M. Since I was already acquainted with the base hospital, I drove there and went straight to the stockroom, borrowed a stainless steel 3-tier cart and loaded it with donuts, sweet buns, etc. I went up and down the ramps and into the hospital wards selling baked goods. The patients loved it and no one stopped me. I wore my vendor's badge on my shirt and everyone thought that I had obtained permission from someone else. I did this for over two years. Shortly before they closed the Air Base, I was called to the administrative office and a new Colonel kicked me out of the hospital. I made a stack of money while it lasted. During that time, Jacqueline was, born. It wasn't long before Terri, Penny and Pam showed up and, finally, along came Thomas. We had six good ones to raise.

Never a Dull Moment

After loosing my business at Sampson, I found a job with Hathaway Bakeries selling baked goods directly to homes. I did this for a prolonged period of time.

The manager, "*Old John*," was a very high strung man and he would get so irate at us drivers that his blood veins would turn purple, threatening to bust out of his neck. For certain, one of us would get fired. Often it was me. I would go home and come back the next day as if nothing had happened, load up my truck and "*Old John*" wouldn't say two words until the next time he fired me.

Sometimes, I wouldn't show up for work the next day after he had fired me and he would send the route supervisor to my home to get me. One time, I took a job delivering baked goods wholesale to stores for another company and another time I delivered milk directly to the homes.

"*Old John*" would always keep calling for me to return and often over the years, I did until the company went belly-up and "*Old John*" died. They buried him belly-up.

A Little More About Our Family

We were always very proud of each of our children, and you can always be proud of your parents. They are the best. We could have never found better children if we had hand picked them ourselves. They were just great as children and are still great as adults. I love each one more dearly than I know how to say. The Fullers' were never good at expressing love. My parents never kissed me or told me that they loved me. I know that they did. My experience has been that showing expressions of love or affection was very uncommon among most farmers and their families. Couples were married for years, and years, seemingly only getting along with each other, without showing affection or love.

I have often wished that I had been able to spend more time with my children as they were growing up, but I was usually working both day and evenings trying to pay the bills. I left Mary in charge and evidently she did one heck of a job. She apparently got a little tired of the job and left home in 1974 and a year later I met Lore. You (my grandchildren), have never known me without Lore, even though it took her ten years to realize what a prize she had and finally married me.

I am going to skip ahead somewhat and tell you about Lore I'll get back to my dull and boring life in Chapter 7

Lore was born, Eleonora Anna Lohninger, in Austria on December 14, 1937. She lived in Austria until she was 17, then moved to Germany where she lived for 5 years. She left Germany in June of 1961 to come to America to marry an American GI that she had met there, but that marriage failed after several years and two children (Mark and Jill). We met in May of 1975 in Syracuse at a club for single parents called, "One Parent Family Council." We were married on February 2, 1985 in Edmeston by Peace Justice, Leon Schworm and left for Florida for a two week honeymoon. In May we flew to Austria to visit her sister and family.

We returned to Austria again in May of 1988. During our visits I enjoyed the beauty of the country, visiting Vienna, Salzburg and Innsbruck as well as southern Germany and northern Italy. Lore has returned several times without me. When I travel with her, she has to devote a great deal of her time translating the German language for me so that I may visit with her people. She likes going alone much better.

Lore's Story

[Or Payton Place Revisited]

With Lore's permission, I want to tell you about her life in Austria and Germany and about a romance that, even though at the time became very distressing and obviously unfortunate, developed into something very positive. It also gives rise to a very interesting story.

The only thing that Lore knows about her father is that he died, in a concentration camp in Mauthausen, Austria, shortly after her birth. He opposed Hitler's Nazi regime and allowed it to be known among the wrong people. Her mother left her with an aunt and uncle but, upon the death of her aunt, she became a ward of the state and was sent to a convent to be raised by nuns. After, what she called two years of torture, being forced to spend many hours on her knees praying, being hungry much of the time and being poorly treated by the nuns she cried, "Uncle" and he came and got her. He brought her back to Frankenmarkt to finish her formal schooling. From there she was sent to Salzburg as an apprentice in the kitchen of a large restaurant to learn cooking. The treatment at cooking school was far worse than the convent, the pay was almost nil and the hours were long and exhausting.

The Americans were occupying Austria in 1955 and one of her friends had found employment as a domestic with an American family. Lore knew that this had to beat cooking school and so she did the same. However, the peace treaty was signed in 1955 and the Americans left. Lore followed an army major's family to Germany and lived in Fuerth, for 5 years. During this time she fell in love with an American GI named, Robert Norman Lynch.

With the promise of wedding bells, an intimate relationship developed and one thing leading to another, Lore found that she was expecting a baby. Robert Lynch was transferred back to the US before the baby was born. He mailed her postcards with the promise that he was returning for her and the baby, however, he never returned. He had been discharged and, as far as Lore knew, he had returned to his home town of Lewistown, PA. She never heard from him again. She had full responsibility for the boy child and after caring for him for 14 months, under extremely stressful circumstances, she took the child to her cousin in Austria and paid her to care for him. His name was Roland. When Roland was two, her cousin advised her that she could no longer care for the child. She and her husband were becoming altogether too fond of him and were fearful that they could not give him up later. They gave Lore an ultimatum: either let them adopt the child or Lore would have to take him back to Germany. She had no way to support Roland and so gave him up for adoption.

In the meantime, she had gone to work at the army post exchange (PX) and had met her future husband whom she married in the US. in 1961. As previously mentioned, this marriage broke up and this is where I came into her life.

A Lost Love Found

[Or The Past Catches Up]

Roland had been told of his parentage and had been visited by his birth mother. I first met Roland when he came to the US to visit Lore and tour the country while on vacation from his college studies. He visited America twice. On the second visit, Lore tried in vain to locate his natural father. She wanted the information in case Roland was interested in meeting him. Roland wasn't inclined to do so and the matter was dropped for the time being.

Lore is a very unusual person. She never harbors ill will of anyone. Even though she had been abandoned in Germany with a baby and in desperate circumstances, and later learning from Robert's commanding officer that he was in fact married and had a family in America and she had been mislead, she still wondered about Bob Lynch. He was Roland's father although he had never seen him or shown any interest in him even though he knew that Roland existed.

In the summer of 1989, Lore and I decided to visit Gettysburg, PA, on our vacation. Before leaving she took the time to look up the town of Lewistown, PA, on the map and discovered that it wasn't very far out of our way to stop there. She thought that with a little detective work on my part, we might be able to find out where this former lover had disappeared to. We arrived in Lewistown late in the evening. We had a little problem locating a motel, as the town is small and motels weren't big on the town's list of buildings. We did find one on the road leading out of town and checked in. We ate some dinner, went back to the motel and started checking names in the phone book. We found a Robert Lynch but no one answered the phone. We also found an R.N. Lynch listed and thought maybe we should take a shot at that name. A man answered and I asked him if he had been stationed in Germany in 1957 and he admitted that he had been. I asked him if the name Eleonora meant anything to him and he said, yes, it did. I asked him if he knew that he had a son and he said yes. I asked him if he would like to see Eleonora and he said that he would. I handed the phone to Lore and the first thing out of his mouth was, "I have been looking for you."

His home was only about two miles south of the motel where we were staying. He was divorced and living alone upstairs, over his boat business, and asked us to come and see him.

Before we had left Syracuse, Lore had gathered up an old album including the pictures and postcards from Bob. We were looking for a tall, good looking American soldier. When we arrived at his home and he came to the door, we both realized what 30 years can do to a person. This old buzzard was older than me and looked it. The first thing out of Lore's mouth was, "Bob, is that you?" He admitted that in 30 years he had put on a little weight and gotten a little older. He invited us into his home and it occurred to us both that this man was much more nervous than we were. He smoked one cigarette after another. We kind of concluded that he wasn't sure why we were there. I am sure that the thought, possibly crossed his mind, that we were after back child support or some compensation.

He apologized for his actions of 30 years ago. He said that he was sorry for leaving her in the bind that he did. He asked Lore to forgive him and she said that she had done that a long time ago or she wouldn't be sitting in his living room now. The emotions were abundant for both of them. He said that he had gone back to Germany and Austria looking for her in the 1960's after he had divorced his wife. We gave him pictures of Roland and his wife and their two children, a girl and a boy (another boy has been born since). It was the first picture that he had seen of his grown son or his grandchildren. [Lore had sent him baby pictures in the early 1960's]. We left them with him and went on our way. We received a letter from him, after we arrived home, telling us how his father lay dying in the hospital and he, too, never knew that he had great grandchildren and was thrilled to see the pictures. The man died a few days later.

Bob has since visited us when he was passing through the Syracuse area, on his way up north to go salmon fishing. Lore received a bouquet of flowers from him at Christmas time. We keep in touch and send him pictures of the Austrian grandchildren as we receive them. The past is past and life goes on. Lore calls Roland from time to time at his home in Innsbruck, Austria. Her cousin is still his mother to him and Lore is a good friend. I think that deep down, Roland feels the natural tie between them as does Lore. In the end it all worked out well.

SEVEN

Back To My Dull and Boring Life

During my working years, I spent most of my time in the sales field. I started selling high quality stainless steel cookware in 1955 and didn't seem to know how to get out of it. It meant working evenings and Saturdays; but every time I tried to get out of working evenings by taking a regular job, the bills would pile up and I always found myself back selling.

As mentioned before, I never knew if my Grandfather had a good day in his life. I never knew if he ever had a good laugh, or if he had ever met anyone interesting. I only remember him as a frail old man that died when I was 9 years old. I want to give you an overview of some of the happenings in my life; some high spots and low spots. Who were some of the people in my life. Working as a salesman almost all of my adult life, I was favored with opportunities to meet people from all walks of life. I had some opportunity to travel which brought me in contact with people that created various incidents. I met some interesting people, had some interesting experiences, had some good times, some sad times, some embarrassing moments, some good laughs; but best of all I watched my family grow to maturity and have children of their own, my grandchildren. At this writing, I even have a great granddaughter.

People, Places and Things

One Fonda That I Am Not To Fond Of

Flying to Columbus, Ohio, in the late 1960's to work, a week or so, with some people selling children's magazines around the state, I had to change planes in Cleveland. I was shouldered out of the way of the famous Jane Fonda by a rather large body guard. She had been in North Vietnam aiding the enemy and was coming back into the United States by way of Canada. She and her entourage were changing planes at the same time and same place as I. Dressed in battle fatigues, she seemed to think that no one was as important as Jane Fonda. It seems that I was standing in her path. I guess that they felt that she was very important as these creeps physically shoved me and several people out of her way, to the boos and catcalls of the more patriotic Americans. I find it very difficult to find a something nice to say about Jane Fonda.

Have a nice day

In 1976 when Atlantic City, NJ, decided to go into the casino business, I was in Philadelphia, Pa working for a company selling chemicals and cleaning supplies. The sales manager, that I was working with, had made a sales appointment with the general manager of the Resorts Hotel. The Resorts was the only casino up and operating at that time and it was extremely busy. The man that we went to see was busy, so we went downstairs to the casino to see how the other half lives. Money was being tossed around like it was monopoly currency. People were lined up at the quarter (one arm bandit) machines and were almost fighting to get in line to get rid of their money. We went over by the craps table and watched a man put down four one hundred dollar bills, roll the dice, lose his four hundred dollars and his only remark was a four letter word as he walked away. Another man was counting out a pile of bills as he put them on the table,1-2-3-4-5-6-7-8-9-10. He picked up the dice, rolled them and lost his stack of bills to the house. At first glance, they looked like $5.00 bills to me but I walked right up to the table, took a good close look, turned around and said to my partner, "Holy Mackerel, Henry, those are fifty's." A big burly man with dark hair came from behind the table and said to me, "You aren't playing, so get out!" Just to show the man what a good sport I was, Henry and I left the building, never to return to the Resorts Hotel again.

The Donner Potatoes

Reflecting on Pennsylvania. One night I was in northern PA working with a fellow cookware salesman, putting on a cookware dinner party demonstration. We usually cooked the potatoes in with the meat to demonstrate our product and on that night we had ham. He had purchased some red potatoes for the meal. Normally the potatoes are done before the ham, but these red potatoes were the hardest things that I had ever seen. I almost think that they were Pennsylvania anthracite coal, painted red to look like potatoes. As we checked the meal and discovered that the potatoes were not fully cooked, he walked into the living room and announced that we would be a little late with the meal as, "We would like to have the potatoes a little more donner." I thought that he was trying to be amusing, but later, after checking the potatoes again, he marched back in and announced, "It will be a little longer before we eat, as I want the potatoes to be a little more donner." After his fourth trip to the living room, with the same "donner" announcement, I knew that our demonstration was for sure a real "donner." I could hear the snickers from the guests everytime he went into his "more donner" speech. I was mortified.

The Pot Party

However, I wasn't as disconcerted with this guy as I was, one night, when I agreed to help a man from Elmira, NY. He had arranged a dinner party demonstration just outside of Watkins Glen, NY. We often joked about our having a "Pot Party" as we were selling pots and pans, but this time it wasn't so amusing. The woman, that was our host, was an older woman and she had invited several neighbors to her "pot party." We were in the middle of our cooking, with all of the guests in the kitchen standing around the stove, as we were explaining the value of cooking in waterless stainless steel cookware. Suddenly the door came flying open and two Sheriff deputies in uniform entered. It seems that someone had tipped them off that a pot party was going on and these boys were going to be local heroes. After showing every kind if identification that we could come up with, and even offering them dinner, they finally backed off without any kind of an apology. The mood of the party became totally negative. Everyone was embarrassed for us and it was almost impossible to complete our job. We did the best that we could and went home. From that day on, we let it be known that, our demonstrations were not to be called pot parties.

Safety First—Keep Your Hands In Your Pocket

I booked a "pot party" at the home of a New York State Trooper south of Syracuse. It was normal to ask the host to invite eight couples, as usually only four couples will show up. It seems that everyone thought that an invitation from a trooper was the same as a summons, because when I called the morning of the demonstration to get the numbers so as to know how many groceries to buy, the man said that he had eight couples coming.

I brought my daughter, Penny, with me to help clean up behind me as I cooked and talked. I did ham and potatoes, and a cake, in one pan. Peas and corn in another, cabbage in another and so on. I made applesauce, to demonstrate the value of waterless cooking, along with coleslaw, to demonstrate a vegetable cutter that had a cylinder cone that one turned by hand to cut the vegetables.

In my haste to get the applesauce started, while the trooper's wife observed the process, I took a small nick out of the end of my finger and it started bleeding profusely. It just wouldn't stop and the guests were on their way into the kitchen to watch the demonstration. As I cut the cabbage on my machine to make the coleslaw, the trooper, whose wife had seen my dilemma and relayed it to him, immediately informed some of the other guests of my predicament. I did my best to hide my finger. I tried to secretly wrap a paper towel around it. Bleeding into the applesauce was not too bad, because I cooked the apples without peeling them and the red jackets blended well with my blood, but the white cabbage was another matter. Penny told me later that she was almost biting her tongue to keep from laughing at her pathetic, frustrated Dad. The life was spurting out of me through a hole in my finger and she thought that it was hilarious. I talked fast, in an attempt to distract everyone, and cut the cabbage and other vegetables as fast as I could, but finally the trooper interrupted me and for the benefit of his guests said, "Can you cut your finger with that thing?"

and I answered, "Yes, but we don't recommend it." Everyone seemed to enjoy my remark. This got me off the hook. Penny told me later, as we were driving home that she was so pleased to be able to finally laugh along with the guests. Her poor father was embarrassed and his very existence was slipping away through an aperture in his finger, and she thought that it was funny. What a sense of humor. It must run in the family.

I Get To Laugh Too

On Labor Day in 1962 or 1963 we were visiting friends, Herb and Shirley Benjamin and their two children. As we were getting ready to start for home, Herb asked me if we liked tomatoes. I answered in the affirmative and he said that he had more in his garden than they could possibly use, so we prepared to pick some. It was dark and the garden was behind his mobile home, so he pulled his car onto the lawn to maneuver the headlights toward the garden. It didn't do much good, but we could see the red tomatoes enough to pick them.

I made mention that he must have a lot of rotten tomatoes, as the smell was overpowering. He said, "Oh, by the way, be careful where you step as there is an open cesspool out heeere..." Splash!

Herb simply disappeared into the darkness and, as fast as he disappeared, he reappeared from a hole in the ground with toilet paper and slime hanging from his ears and the smell was multiplied to the point of being staggering. Herb, somehow, made it out of the hole and ran to the children's wading pool and jumped in head first. I couldn't stop laughing. I laughed so hard that I hurt. I could never have helped the poor guy out of that hole, as I was laying down on the ground in pain from guffawing so hard.

Herb had dug a hole in the ground in the spring, meaning to put in a septic system. He just never got around to doing it. The result was that all of the waste water and raw sewage from the toilet ran into the hole. The tomatoes had grown over the top of the hole during the summer and kept out the odor much like any cover might. Herb had simply forgotten about the hole, until we went to pick tomatoes in the dark. It's a wonder that the gasses didn't kill the poor guy, but I am grateful that they didn't, because I was just heehawing too hard to be able to help pull slimy Herb out of that hole.

The Copycat

I had a similar experience with a fellow salesman in Cleveland, Ohio. I had gone to Cleveland to work with a sales group that had a new line of cutlery that would compliment my cookware package. I stayed in a motel on Euclid Ave. for several days. We would meet in the morning

for a sales meeting and from there we would go prospecting.
I was working with a young man named Tony. He lived just
outside of Cleveland and so we made calls in his
neighborhood.

We had an appointment in the evening with a young couple
who had recently moved into a large mobile home that they
had set up on their own lot. It was daylight when we arrived.
As we entered the mobile home, we noticed a rather large
hole directly in front of the steps that led us into the home.
The hole had about 6 or 8 inches of water in the bottom and
it smelled stagnant. The couple explained that the hole had
been dug for a septic tank but, that the inspectors had forced
them to set the tank farther away from the home. The
workers were supposed to fill in the hole the Friday before
but, because of the heavy rain on that day, they were unable
to and promised to return early in the week to finish the job.
They hadn't returned. We went on with our sales pitch and
after making the sale, thanked them for their order and left.
Fortunately, I was carrying the sales kit and the order
because as we walked out the door into the dark of the
night, I heard a rather loud splash and a man yelling, "Get
me out of here."

Tony had stepped off the little porch and dropped about 6
feet into the stagnant water. He hadn't even taken the time
to remove his shoes, suit or necktie. I thought, "What a
showoff." Our new customer grabbed a flashlight and

directed the beam into the hole at Tony. He sure did look funny to me splashing around in that muddy hole fully clothed. The woman was almost hysterical but I was laughing my silly head off. I just couldn't stop laughing and the more I laughed the louder poor Tony shouted.

We couldn't get him out by ourselves, so the man ran down the road to the neighbors and borrowed a ladder. Tony was able to crawl out on his own power. The couple let Tony have an old towel to wrap around him and he drove me back to the motel. He didn't say much all the way home, but he was okay the next morning at the sales meeting and we worked together the rest of the week. Selling can be fun if you work with the right people.

Selling Can Be Embarrassing Too

One afternoon I received a call from a girl who had purchased some china and cookware earlier and now wanted to get her crystal. I made an appointment for that afternoon when she would be home from work at about 5:30. I carried all of my samples in a large suitcase. After showing her my samples, in her dining room, I was writing up the order when a car pulled into the driveway. The girl said, "Hurry you must leave." She explained to me that it was her boyfriend who had just driven into the driveway, and he didn't want her to buy any crystal. I handed her the contract to sign and literally threw my samples into the suitcase, grabbed her down payment money and headed for the door.

Since I had parked out in front of the house, I headed for the front door before the boyfriend had time to get in the backdoor. As the backdoor opened, I went out the front door. Only, in my distress, as I shut the door behind me, I realized that I had gone into the girl's bedroom.

Now what do I do? I thought maybe I should go out the window onto the porch and escape, but what if a police car came by or anyone else for that matter. What if I couldn't get the window open? I had to think fast. Should I hide under the bed? Not a good idea! I was just full of questions as to what to do, so I did the only sensible thing left to do. I turned around and walked out of the girl's bedroom, suitcase and all.

The couple were in an embrace. I looked at the young man and simply said, "Hi," as I walked out the front door, got into my car and made my escape. I had her order shipped via UPS and I never braved going back to find out how she explained to her boyfriend what this guy was doing coming out of her bedroom with a large suitcase.

Who Said There Is No Free Lunch

At one time selling World Book Encyclopedias was widespread and I sold my share. At times it became necessary to go door to door looking for prospects. One day I was in the city of Syracuse going door to door, when a young girl that I had never seen before came to the door and said, "Well hi, how are you today? Gee, I've never seen you dressed up with a necktie and jacket before. You sure do look nice. Come on in."

I was a little overwhelmed at the extraordinary reception and somewhat puzzled, but I went into the house certain that I was going to have a sale here. She had a couple of kids and they were sitting at the kitchen table eating hot dogs and drinking a Pepsi. She said, "Won't you join us, we are just having some lunch. Here, have a hot dog and a Pepsi." So I had a hot dog and Pepsi.

She was just about the friendliest thing that I had ever seen and I wondered if, maybe, I knew her from somewhere. She asked me what I was doing in the city on my day off and how surprised and pleased she was to see me today. I couldn't place her in my mind from anywhere, but I was enjoying my hot dog and Pepsi, when there was a knock at the back door. It was the girl that lived upstairs. My very friendly and pleasant host said to her neighbor, 'Hi, come on, I want you to meet my milkman." In those days milk was still being delivered to the door, by what else but a milkman. I began to realize that there was a milkman in Syracuse that looked like me. Probably not as modest or as handsome, but close enough to confuse this pretty young thing.

The neighbor girl indicated that she too wanted service and wanted me to start delivering her milk just as soon as possible. I took her milk order. I thanked my host for the lunch and as they say, "I made tracks." I didn't want to stick around. I know of a man that was arrested for impersonating a police officer. I wasn't sure what the penalty was for impersonating a milkman.

I didn't canvass that area again. I have often wondered what happened when the regular milkman didn't deliver the neighbor's order. I have to think that she must have mentioned to him the lovely visit that they had the day before. I am not sure who might have been the most embarrassed, me, the young mother or the milkman.

A Distorted View

One day I stopped at a new McDonald's for lunch and went into the men's room to wash my hands. As I turned on the water, the pressure was such that the water hit the basin and splashed out all over the front of my pants. I felt that it might look a little strange for a grown man to leave the washroom with the front of his pants soaked. I decided to solve the problem by turning on the hot air blower normally used to dry your hands. By standing on my toes and pulling my trousers up to the blower, I could tell that the water was slowly disappearing and that my pants were starting to dry. I was so engrossed in my work that I was thinking of nothing else. The door opened and a well dressed man walked into the men's room. He took one look at me, turned and walked back out, not saying a word or giving me a chance to explain. I was so embarrassed that I didn't stay for lunch. I walked out of the door, went to my car and drove away. I am sure that that man went back to his office and told everyone that he had seen a pervert making love to the hand dryer.

A Spectacle

In 1954 when I was delivering baked goods to homes, I had the route that took me over to Watkins Glen and Horseheads, NY. We were living in Enfield, west of Ithaca, and Mary was expecting Terri. Since I could easily go by the house on my way back to the office, I would often stop and pick up groceries as I was working six days a week and usually didn't get home until late. One afternoon, I stopped at the brand new Grand Union Supermarket in Horseheads. It was their grand opening and the store was extremely busy. I had four brown paper bags full of groceries and asked the bag boy to lift the bags into my arms. I hugged them to my chest as I was leaving the store. I walked to the nice new glass double doors and turned around to push the door open with my rump.

I had never seen and I had never heard of automatic doors. These were new and just becoming popular, but not popular enough for me to have had any experience with them. Now when one goes to push the door with one's derriere, resistance is expected. When there is no resistance there is the tendency to loose your balance. Since you are moving backwards and trying to catch your balance, you tend to pick up speed in reverse. Eventually this speed becomes an awkward back-stepping dance and suddenly everything falls apart. You are no longer back stepping, you are suddenly in a sitting position in the middle of a supermarket parking lot with busted bags and groceries laying all around you.

I gathered up the groceries and tossed them into the truck as fast as I could. I felt that the fewer people that saw me the better I liked it. I never went back to the Horseheads Supermarket again, but I did learn how to use automatic doors.

One Leg Up

One of my jobs at the Ithaca Journal Newspaper, was to make out the payroll for our route delivery people. We paid our route drivers in cash. Every Friday morning after figuring out how much cash would be needed, I would requisition a check and take the check to the Tompkins County Trust Company Bank in Ithaca to cash it. One morning as I stood in line a young woman joined the line next to me. She had a small poodle dog on a leash. Even in 1960 dogs weren't allowed in banks unless they were depositors. This one was. Standing in front of the woman were two men dressed in suits discussing the value of whole life insurance over the cheaper term policies. These two men were so absorbed in their discussion that they failed to notice the dog as he lifted his hind leg and, apparently thinking that the man's pant leg was a fire hydrant, let fly. The woman noticed the quandary that she was in and soon unearthed her solution. She left the bank with her dog. It took a few moments for the water that had come from the warm water outlet to turn cold. The man looked down at his pant leg. He looked around the bank. He lifted his pant leg. He looked in his shoe. To this day, this man is still wondering how his shoe became full of water while standing in the teller's line at the Tompkins County Trust company.

Two Legs Down

Dogs always make great pets. They always seem to know what to do, and when to do it. One evening I was in a country home selling encyclopedias. Since it is impossible to carry around a 22 volume encyclopedia set on sales calls, we used a broadside. The broadside was made of heavy weight paper, about 3 feet by 4 feet, and it illustrated the encyclopedias in all of their picturesque grandeur.

The sales call consisted of showing a prospectus. This gave an overview of the entire set of encyclopedias with the actual sales pitch included. Next came the A volume to show an actual book, followed by the broadside to demonstrate the size and beauty of the set.

I had come to the point of showing the broadside. I had it nicely covering a significant portion of the living room floor and, returning to the prospectus, had come to the most important part of the presentation, called the sales close. I was so engrossed in this consequential part of my performance that I failed to see the family's new puppy creeping into the living room. I was about to lower the boom and close the sale, when the woman of the house let out a shriek that quickly got my attention. The puppy was being paper trained and the cute little fellow had found a paper. He was so proud of his day's work. On top of my beautiful broadside was a pile of puppy poop. I have often wondered whether the puppy was actually being house trained or if he had been educated solely for this purpose.

Bob The Bell Ringer

Robert Shaw retired from the U.S. army as a Lt. Colonel. He moved to Ithaca with his wife and two boys and started attending the Nazarene Church where my father-in-law was pastor. He had taken a job on a farm, while finishing his education at Cornell University on the GI Bill and later went on to teaching school for a few years. We became very good friends. His wife and Mary also became very good friends and so we spent some time together, usually on a Sunday afternoon. I enjoyed listening to his life story.

Bob had disappeared from Syracuse University as a freshman and left Syracuse for the mid-west. There he got a job working in a bakery. He had learned the baking trade fairly well, when an army colonel came by and asked him to join the army and work as the base baker. This was in the 1930's. With no basic training, he immediately became a buck private in the US Army and went to work as the base baker. Through the years he had acquired some basic training in bits and pieces, but he was always associated with the mess halls. He worked his way from private to a Lt. Colonel over the years.

After World War II, he was stationed in Japan. I guess that you would call him the "mess" officer as he had charge of all the mess halls on the base where he was stationed.

We were invited to his home for dinner one Sunday after church. Bob and I were wandering around outside his house, while the women were preparing dinner, when I noticed a very large bell hanging from a big tree. I noticed that there wasn't any clapper inside the bell and I asked Bob about it. He told me how he had purchased the bell while on duty in Japan. He explained that the writing on the bell meant something in Japanese and that the bell had an unusually beautiful tone when struck correctly. He went on to explain that to ring the bell, one only had to strike it with a large stick. He kept a big heavy stick underneath the bell solely for this purpose. As he proceeded to demonstrate to me the proper way to ring his bell, he bent down to pick up the stick and in raising up too quickly his head struck the bell extremely hard.

There was a very loud "**Bong.**" I must say that the tone was magnificent. The poor colonel was on his knees holding his head in his hands, in severe pain. So was I in pain from laughing. Finally, I was able to remark how beautiful the bell sounded and, "Would you ring it again?"

His wife, on the other hand, had heard all of the bell ringing that she wanted to hear and she came to the kitchen window and shouted out, "Bob, stop ringing that bell." I don't think that Bob needed the scolding from his wife or my hysterics. The large "goose egg" on his head was reminder enough that the bell was in good working order.

When we were invited to dinner on another occasion, I remarked that we would be glad to come if Bob would promise not to ring his bell. I never heard that bell ring again.

Bill and the Earthquake

At one time, while selling cookware, I had a sales manager by the name of Bill Briggs. Bill and I enjoyed very much working together. We would often share our sales, taking turns doing the demonstrations. We had hired two new salesmen at Christmas time. Knowing how difficult it is to work around home during dead week (the week between Christmas and New Year's), we decided to take the new recruits to Oneonta, NY, and train them in that city. We rented two adjoining rooms at a motel, putting the new trainees in one room while Bill and I shared the other. Bill liked to watch television in bed. That was okay, but he always fell asleep leaving it on. About 2 o'clock in the morning, I would be awakened by the loud humming of the test pattern on the TV and would get up and shut it off. That was all right the first night. I mentioned it to him and he assured me that it wouldn't happen again. It did the next night and also the third night.

When we had checked into the motel rooms, we had discovered that one of the beds was a vibrator bed. The purpose was to relax one after a hard day's work or travel. All you had to do was insert a quarter in a little slot, and you got the ride of your life.

On the third night, when the test pattern came on and Bill was sleeping ever so peacefully, feeling a little contemptible, I put a quarter in the slot of Bill's vibrator bed. The hullabaloo that he raised, as he jumped out of that bed should have awakened the dead. It took myself and the two new recruits several minutes to settle him down. For some reason, Bill was convinced that we were all going to "*buy the farm*" in the Oneonta earthquake. We didn't work together for an extended period of time after that. Poor sport!

We Buy Nothing At The Door

Salesmen and peddlers have been around, most likely, since the beginning of time. Some people just don't know what to make of them. Every time a salesman calls, a red flag goes up. The red flag is a warning to the individual that he, or she, is considered a prospect and is actually going to face a challenge. Only one person is going to prevail. It may be the salesperson, or it may be the prospect. Some are so fearsome of the challenge that they prefer not to deal with it. This means only one thing. Get rid of the salesperson before he, or she, can get their foot in the door. This isn't always easy. Salespeople, not infrequently, have an enterprising way of being assertive. Before one realizes what has happened, the salesperson is sitting in the living room, or at the kitchen table, making an offer that is at times just too difficult to resist. You find yourself craving a product that only a few minutes earlier you may not have even known existed. If the salesperson prevails, the prospect is now the proud new owner of an eye-popping, spine tingling product which the prospect has realized he, or she, absolutely can't live without.

In the mid-1960's a salesman made his way throughout the city of Cortland, NY selling, of all things, unattractive little two sentence signs that could be placed next to the door bells, or knockers, that read, "We buy absolutely nothing at the door— Salesmen are not welcome."

Bill Briggs, my manager, and I had decided to meet and work in the city of Cortland before we knew about these wonderful little additions to the homes. At first they seemed to work. When a door was answered, the prospect would simply point at the sign and ask us if we could read. After a couple of disappointments, we decided that we needed to master the approach. We knew that removing the little bugger would only infuriate the prospect. We had to gain the prospect's trust and confidence. We came to the decision that we should admire the troublesome, insignificant, little notices and compliment the prospect on their extraordinary purchase. This way we could, at least, start some kind of a dialogue with them. It worked.

We soon found ourselves selling more sets of cookware in Cortland than ever before. Bill had an explanation. He was convinced that these people knew, that if a salesman ever made it into their home, they would in all probability become a buyer. This is sometimes referred to as apprehension, alarm or, more candidly, fear. Thus the theory to keep the salesperson on the outside of the door by any and all means accessible.

After this experience, Bill convinced me that, anytime such a notice was posted on or near a home, a sale would be inevitable. I was a confirmed believer.

The Zealot

Knowing that only the weak and fearful resorted to affixing notices for salesmen not to bother even trying to come closer than the "no salesmen allowed" proclamation, I began looking for just such declarations. It didn't take long to find various versions.

Working in the rural area near the small town of Freeville, NY, I happened upon a rather easy sale and the couple freely gave me a referral list of people to go and see. Before leaving the home, I called one of the referrals and made an appointment to see them. The drive to the home took me a little over 30 minutes, but when I arrived the couple was not there. The home was a small house trailer. A gravel driveway led to the trailer and about 30 feet on the other side of the driveway stood an old shack. The shack looked deserted, but as I approached the trailer I noticed three things. Number one was the small notice reading, "We buy nothing at the door—Salesmen not welcome." Number two, the same notice could be seen on the old shack and, number three, the shack door was now open and a man was standing in front of it. The man had no teeth, just a fringe of hair and a nose that remeined me of a hawk. His eyes were beady, little things that seemed to be hidden behind his hawk-like beak. The man not only was not pleasant to look at but he certainly wasn't pleasant to talk to either. The first words out of his mouth were, "Can't you read?" I assured him that I could. I assured him that I had not come to see him and, further, I had an appointment with the people that lived in the trailer. He advised me that it was his daughter and her husband that lived in the trailer and that I should, "Get!" I may have been a little overconfident. I knew that I had an appointment. I knew that the notice regarding salesmen was a positive sign of weakness and, I was convinced, that I had a sale at this dwelling if only I could locate the owner.

While contemplating my next move, I heard the order to, "Get!" I was facing a man of few words and his favorite word was, "Get." Well, I didn't "get." I demanded to know where my prospect was. He demanded that I, "Get!" Without warning, a stone went flying past my head. Unexpectedly, a second stone went flying past my head. Abruptly, I did as commanded, "I get!"

The Fanatic

On a warm summer afternoon, I was working out in the rural area somewhere beyond the village of Slaterville Springs. This was real country. I discovered that some of the houses were no more than weather worn shacks. I had a referral in my pocket and I was determined to find the prospect, make a sale. As I was driving down a side road, I came across an old farm house with a hand painted sign that read, "No Salesmun Aloud." Now I ask you, how could I go wrong. This was, indisputably an easy sale if I ever saw one.

I directed my car into what tentatively might be called a driveway and parked it about a 100 meters from the house. I walked to the front door and knocked. No answer. I knew that these people were home, but they were not going to answer the door. They may have come to the conclusion that a salesman was at their door. Now it would be a contest of wills. I knew that I was the skilled professional here. I gave the door a whack that should get their attention. No answer. I heard the back door creaking open. Ah ha, so they were sneaking out the back door. These people were really apprehensive about meeting salesmen. I was convinced that, if I could get their attention, in all likelihood, I would have an easy transaction.

No way were these people going to get away from me. I stepped off the front porch and started toward the rear of the house, when out of nowhere, at an accelerated speed, came the biggest, ugliest canine that I had ever seen. The only safe haven was my car, 100 meters away.

In 1936 at the Olympic Games in Berlin, Germany, a black man, Jessie Owens, humiliated Adolph Hitler and his Nazis, by winning four Olympic Gold Medals. He earned one by running the 100 meter dash in 10.3 seconds. I did it in 10.2 seconds. The dog did it in 10.1 seconds. I stood up while driving home.

The Dog and the Crystal

Driving back toward home in Ithaca from Cortland one evening, I drove out into the country near the town of McGraw. I had a prospect back on one of the farms. Even though it was getting late, I felt that perhaps, I should chance it and try to make one more sales presentation.

I was calling on a young girl in an attempt to sell her some cookware, china and/or crystal for what we called a Hope Chest. The girl was home as was her mother. I didn't know, at the time, that the father had gone to bed for the night. When it came time to demonstrate the high quality of the crystal that I was attempting to sell, I wet my finger and slid it around the edge of the tumbler to bring out the singing that is associated with fine crystal. There seems to be times when the crystal will sing louder and clearer than at other times. This was a night for loud and clear. As the crystal sang, so did the family dog. Only, the dog wasn't singing, he was crying. The loud singing of the crystal was hurting his ears. The loud crying of the dog and the crystal soon brought Dad bounding down the stairs demanding to know what was going on. He was as surprised at seeing me in his living room with his wife and daughter, as I was seeing him running down the stairs in his night clothes. Let me explain exactly what salesmanship is. Most people have the erroneous notion that salesmanship is simply selling a product. Salesmanship, at its finest, is calming down a distraught farmer who has been awakened from a deep sleep, explaining my presence in his living room with his wife and daughter, and sending him back to bed so that I can *simply* sell my product.

I Need Your Opinion

As a sales manager, I was required to run ads for salesmen. When they answered the ad I would call them into my office for an interview. Actually, I would kind of check to see if they had a pulse. If they appeared to be breathing regularly and the heart was ticking, they were hired on the spot, on a commission basis. I would do the training.

I hired a young man and took him with me for his first evening of training. I had several leads in the Cortland area. We had made several calls and the evening was not, what you would call flourishing. I had a prospect near Cortland, a farm girl who was working at the Cortland Bank. Darkness was settling in and my recruit thought that we were going home over some back road. He was in for a total surprise. Cookware salesmen work half the night sometimes.

I located the farm, talked to the girl and asked if I might share a few minutes with her to show her some new and exciting things. Back then, the age of majority was twenty one. My prospect was only twenty. This meant that I would need the signature of an adult on the credit contract, if the girl was to make a purchase. Thus, I said to her mother, "I would like very much for you to join us, as I really would like your opinion." This approach, frequently made the mother feel that her opinion was exceptional, and the mother, generally, would guide the daughter in my direction when it came time for the close. Most mothers had, at one time or another, wanted something this magnificent. The general rule was, get the mother involved. Often this resulted in two sales. Not this night.

As I was making my sales presentation, the father came in from the barn. He said that he had been putting his cows to bed and sat down in a chair in the living room to join us. The mother said to him that it was past his bed time, and that he should go upstairs to bed. Without one word, he got up from his chair and went directly to bed. I knew who ran that family.

My first thought was, great, one less opinion to overcome. Now it was just the daughter, Ma, and me. I knew that I could handle this little group. I came to the close. The girl was excited and overjoyed with the combination package of cookware, china and crystal that I had put together for her.

I had finished writing up an absolutely delightful, large order and was handing it to the girl for her signature when an unanticipated roar came from the direction of the girl's mother.

The mother accused me of being a no good traveling salesman. She said that I really didn't care a hoot about her daughter and was only interested in getting my hands on her money. She accused her daughter of being foolish, asinine and stupid to even think of signing that paper. This woman went on and on like a maniac. After she finished with her daughter, [who now was crying], and after she finished with me, [who now felt like crying], she turned to my new sales recruit. This poor guy hadn't said two words all evening, but he was with me and she let him have it. After she slowed down enough for him to say something, he explained to her that he was just hitch-hiking to Cortland and that I had picked him up, and he was just along for the ride. It's difficult to keep salesmen at times.

The Professor's Wife

There are times when a salesman is just as well off if he stays home. That way he doesn't face humiliation or embarrassment. He knows that he isn't going to make any money either, on the other hand, going to work as there is no guarantee that a sale is to be made.

One evening, I had been given the name and address of a Cornell University Professor's daughter as a referral. My first conviction was to toss the lead away as this girl, in all probability, would be going to college and college girls are not exceptional prospects. Since I didn't have a stack of leads to work with on this particular evening, I decided that I would drive up to Cayuga Heights and make the call.

I explained to the girl that I was there to sell her, what we called, hope chest items for her future home. She was a delightful young woman and was eager to see my merchandise. I gave my usual, "I would like your opinion" speech to the mother and she agreed to join us.

We were in the living room. I had the coffee table well strewn with my samples and was making one of my better sales presentations when, out of nowhere, came a loud squeaking noise similar to air being let out of a balloon with the opening being stretched. This was followed by a fragrance of a rather powerful proportion that, to say the least, was not a pleasing experience.

I completely ignored this minor incident and continued with my presentation. I was in mid-sentence when again, I was interrupted by an extremely loud reverberating sound. I was aware that the noise was coming from the direction of the mother but, being the polished gentleman that I am, I simply attempted to ignore it. The bouquet was just to powerful too ignore. I did my best to keep a straight face. I was amused, but embarrassed. I had never been required to do business with anything like this before.

I had decided that it might be best, for all concerned, if I made my close. Before I could get the sales contract out of my sales kit, we were visited by another resounding eruption, similar to a crack of thunder. The room was soon filled with an obnoxious odor that would make a more delicate person keel over. The daughter, being a woman of good breeding, simply said, "Mother."

Mother, being a cultured woman, reached over to the coffee table and started packing up my sales kit for me. I was somewhere between gnawing on my tongue to keep from laughing, to crying from the pungency of the personal blunders that had interrupted my performance, to complete embarrassment. I know that the daughter was embarrassed. I was embarrassed. Mother, well, she just kept packing up my sales kit.

Other People Get Embarrassed Too

When we first moved to Ithaca back in the 1950's, there was a small country store located on Danby Road, owned by a man named Walker Smith. Walker was the kind of man that you could sit and talk with, and at times I did. Walker had earned a reputation. Some people said that he had a little larceny in him, but Walker always countered with the reality that everyone had a little larceny in them. He always said that he was as honest as he could afford to be.

Walker related one story to me that I thought that you might find interesting. He had an old ice cream freezer in his store, that he would place meat in to freeze before it spoiled in the meat case. He had placed his last small chicken in the freezer and was ready to close up. It was on a Saturday night. Before he had a chance to lock the door, one of his regular customers came in wanting to buy a chicken. She told Walker that she was having company on Sunday and wanted his largest chicken. Walker related how he placed the lonely chicken on the scales and quoted her the pound and the price. The woman didn't think that the chicken was big enough and asked if he had a larger one. Walker acknowledged to me that he placed the lonely chicken back into the freezer. Digging around the bottom of the freezer, as if looking for another chicken, he retrieved the same chicken placing it on the scale along with his thumb. Now a four pound chicken weighed five pounds. Walker told me that the lady studied the scale for a few moments and then said, "You know Walker, I think that I'll take both chickens."

EIGHT

Life Has Its Difficulties and Its Rewards

I wanted to cease working evenings and that would require getting a day job that could support our large family. I tried managing an appliance store but found myself still going out in the evenings selling either cookware or encyclopedias. I finally took a job with the Industrial Division of Fuller Brush. We were required to move from Ithaca to Syracuse. This we did and I traveled throughout Central New York calling on large industries and schools. I wasn't earning enough money to pay our bills and found myself going back out evenings selling encyclopedias. This took its toll on the family as I wasn't home very much and Mary apparently couldn't handle taking so much of the family responsibility. One thing led to another and she left home. At about the same time, Fuller Brush was sold to Consolidated Foods and I lost my job. I went back into the cookware business demonstrating the product through the dinner party program.

The Chemical Salesman

Working evenings wasn't an option with three kids still at home, so I applied for a job advertised in the newspaper for a company selling chemicals. There was a room full of applicants. We were all required to take both an attitude and an aptitude test. This took about three hours and the questions were totally ridiculous. For example, several questions related to fishing and golfing and public speaking. The questions would sound very much alike but put in different ways so as to trip you up if, by chance, one was trying to figure out the purpose of such foolish questions.

One question was: What would you rather do.1.Fish for sport. 2. Fish for a living. 3. Sell chemicals. Somehow I had the strange idea that the company might be looking for a chemical salesman not a fisherman, and I out and out lied and marked number 3. Wouldn't anyone in his right mind rather sell chemicals than go fishing? Apparently most of the men didn't think so as I got the job. Less than four years later the company went bankrupt. I think that most of the salesmen spent their time fishing instead of selling.

Hi Tech Chemicals

I had sold life insurance in Ithaca for a couple of years back in the mid-1960's so, I reactivated my license and went to work for The Prudential. Again, it was evening work, I was now single and I could find all kinds of wonderful things to do with my evenings. After a few months, I landed a job with another chemical company and went back to working days. I had a predicament. I knew that I was in over my head. This company was a specialty chemical company, and I knew nothing about specialty chemicals. This was high tech stuff.

Every morning I had to meet my manager and another salesman named Charlie, at a restaurant in Syracuse. After coffee we would go to work. Let's put it another way, we were supposed to go to work. Charlie and I would meet at another restaurant, have more coffee and wonder, how in the world, we would survive the day. Charlie was in over his head too.

One cold, January day, I sold some water treatment powder to a large warehouse. The powder was sold by the pound and I quoted the product by the gallon. I insisted that the company needed X number of gallons and the purchase order was granted on that basis. When I called the order in to the home office, I was advised of my mistake and that the order total came to well over $3,000 instead of a little over the $200.00 that I had quoted. I immediately called the office of the warehouse and advised the buyer's assistant of my error, telling her that I would need to get a new purchase order. She advised me that she had no intention of typing up a new purchase order and, since the total price was not mentioned on the original purchase order and that it was already signed by the purchase officer in charge, to just let it go through. I did. The chemical company was elated with such a nice large order.

I was a little nervous as to how loud the purchasing officer would scream when he received his bill. At this time I was living alone, Tom and Pam were both in college, Penny was living in the Boston area and Ray, Jackie and Terri were all married. So I figured that maybe it was time for a little vacation. I called my two sisters in Florida (Pauline and Barbara) and told them that I was on my way.

I was only gone for two weeks and, when I returned, I went to the restaurant as if it was just another work day. As expected, there was my manager along with Charlie and another man whom I had never met. The boss asked me where I had been for the past two weeks. I told him, "Florida." He said, "Why wasn't I advised that you were going to Florida?" I replied, "I didn't know that you wanted to go." He declared that I had been fired and was being replaced by this man that I had never met. I uttered, "Well, I'll be darned." I asked him if he would mind paying for my coffee since I didn't have a job. He did mind!

Charlie met me for coffee at our usual hideaway and told me that, after I left, the boss said, "That Fuller is a strange duck, isn't he? First he's here and then he's gone and then he's here again." I suppose it is better to be a strange duck than a silly goose, but I still had living expenses to meet so I answered a "blind" ad for a salesman.

Never Answer A *Blind* Ad

Shortly after applying for a "sales position" by writing, c/o the local newspaper, I received a phone call from Waco, Texas and the man announced, "Do I have a deal for you." He went on to explain that it would be in my utmost interest to fly to Waco and visit the company headquarters and to plan on at least three days.

I figured that this must be some big company since I once was invited to fly out to visit the Spangeler Candy Company factory in Bryan, Ohio, at their expense for an interview and to tour the candy factory. I only spent two days there and they are a big company. After some negotiation he agreed to pay my expenses. I was to fly out that Sunday so I would have to buy my own airline ticket but they would reimburse me when I got to Waco. I paid the $800.00 plus for the two-way ticket and flew to Dallas, via Chicago, on Sunday morning. I landed at the Dallas Airport in the late afternoon and was advised, at the information desk, that the funny sounding air carrier with a Mexican name that I was to take to Waco could be reached only by taking the tram.

I rode that tram for what seemed like hours. I was sure that this thing was taking me to Mexico but it finally stopped. The automated conductor told all of us that remained on the tram that this was the last stop and we should exit. And exit we did. There were a dozen other pilgrims like myself standing out in an open field wondering where we were. A man came up to us and said to come this way. We followed him to a clapped out, old school bus and he directed us to get in. And get in we did. He drove some distance before we finally saw, out in the middle of a makeshift runway, a small propeller-driven airplane that looked like it might run on rubber bands. We had just departed from a 737 and this thing looked grotesque. I stayed back, as the other dozen people got into the plane, hoping that there just might be some mistake and that perhaps, God, or the Green Hornet, might come to my rescue. It didn't happen, I was told to get into the airplane. Inside, I found only one seat available. It was a little jump seat at the back of the plane and two rows of double seats held the other twelve passengers. I was number 13. I knew that I was not flying first- class.

In front of the twelve other passengers sat the pilot and the co-pilot who doubled as the navigator and stewardess. My only hope of surviving this flight was the pilot. I surely hoped that he loved his life enough to get us to Waco. The pilot pretended to be talking into a microphone (*we all knew that it was a fake*) while he and his partner started pushing buttons and pulling levers. After a roar of the engines we were headed down a little bumpy runway and soon were airborne. We made it to Waco and I had the urge to kiss the ground, until I remembered that this was Texas soil and I still had some dignity left. So I simply followed the group to the building where I was met by a very well dressed man who loaded me into his Cadillac and took me to a motel.

It turned out that this was not a *job* interview. The company was selling *opportunities.* I was being offered an opportunity to get rich, selling their self-improvement books and tapes, by buying into the business itself. There were about thirty poor imbeciles like myself who had taken the bait and flown to Waco from around the country. We were to have a three day seminar to learn how to work this program and, since we had no other choice, we decided to take an active part. Actually, it was quite informative and I did learn a great deal. I can't remember just what it was that I learned except to be more cautious in the future regarding job advertisements.

A Texas Barbecue

It was on the second day that the Texas boys took us all out for a good old fashioned Texas Barbecue. We all piled into several Cadillacs and we were driven, to somewhere in the Waco area, to a big old barn. I mean a big old Texas size barn. It was an indoor barbecue complete with picnic tables and open barbecue pits and nothing to eat except ribs, ribs, and more ribs.

In one corner was a pile of bones about the size of the State of New Jersey and, everywhere you looked, there were good old Texas boys with huge hats and cowboy boots and one could hear the Texas drawl as they chewed and talked. These boys were gnawing on those ribs like they were going out of fashion. Some were gnawing and tossing, some were only nibbling and tossing. We all watched with fascination as the bone pile grew larger and larger as we got in line for our dinner.

I never was much of a rib man so I hoped to get a steak or something with a little more promise. It seems that Texas steers only have ribs. No steaks. We kind of got the attention of the Texas boys in a hurry. Here was a bunch of shiny shoed salesmen dressed in Sunday go-to-meeting clothes, real neckties instead of strings, real suit jackets instead of vests and none of us had a hat. Apparently the ultimate insult was when a couple of us inquired about the possibility of getting something besides ribs. We were quietly advised by our hosts to order the specialty of the house and so we did. We sat down with our ribs and something they called Texas Cole Slaw. We called it large hunks of cabbage chopped up with a machete with some vinegar poured into it to give it a little kick. We did our share of chewing and tossing and made our exit.

Buying a Job & Getting Home

After our three day seminar we were advised that the cost of buying into the program was $800.00. The cost of my plane ticket. I advised my sponsor that I wasn't interested in self-improvement and he advised me that he wasn't going to reimburse me for my air fare. He insisted that the $800.00 air fare that I had paid would cover the cost of the program and called it an even swap. I called it a rip off. After some hot-tempered negotiations, I was able to recover half of my money but I was still facing that flight back to the Dallas Airport on the little windup toy that they called an airplane. Some of us tried to hire a limo service or rent a car to get us to Dallas, but nothing was available so we had no choice.

One of the other chumps in the group was to make the same connections in Dallas as I was so we flew together to Dallas. As we got into the plane we made certain not to get the jump seat so we commandeered the two back seats. In front of us were two very well dressed Texas businessmen in their elegant business suits, that made our Sears suits look like something we might have purchased off of the Rescue Mission rack. To the right of the two gentlemen sat a teen-aged girl with her mother. As the plane took off it shook and shimmied, left the ground, got tossed around a little bit by a small air current that was caused when a Texas goose flew past, and the girl quickly filled her barf bag with her breakfast. She handed the bag to her mother and reached over to retrieve the bag that was across the aisle in front of one of the Texas businessmen. I think that it was last night's supper that came flying up and out all over the man's expensive suit. The plane smelled of vomit. The man was raving, the girl was crying and I was yearning for Syracuse.

737's Can Be Bumpy Too

I was so happy to get on that big old 737 and head for New York City and on to Syracuse. Everything was just fine. We were offered a choice of food from the menu and I ordered the steak that I couldn't get in Texas. For airline food it was all right but, all of a sudden, we hit turbulence. The plane went down for a way and suddenly it would go from side to side and back up again. I was beginning to understand how that poor girl felt on the first leg of my trip. The only difference was I was not going to throw up, I was going to throw down. Diarrhea has no place on an airplane, especially when you are sitting at the window seat and have to crawl over two guys to get to the aisle, then run the length of the airplane to the "*privy*" only to find both of them full. When one finally became available I immediately staked my claim. As the plane continued to pitch and dive I was hanging onto the toilet seat with both hands and the consommé was slapping me on my buttocks. The stewardess was pounding at the door, demanding that I return to my seat. I informed her that I was in my seat and that I really needed to stay here. Finally, when I was empty and dizzy I made it back to my seat. I was so weak that I didn't stir until we landed in Syracuse. I have never been back to Texas and, by the Grace of God, I never shall.

Old Age Sets In

I worked as a bill collector for Syracuse Cable Company for a little over four years, and after the company was sold I went back to direct selling. One morning I woke up and found myself getting old; They informed me that I was a senior citizen.

Senior citizens are us more mature people who have been there and done that. One starts to loose hair, the eyes get dim and you go to trifocals. I have my own teeth, or at least they will be mine when I make the last payment. I knew that my hearing was going a little, but the real test came one evening at an awards banquet given for a friend of ours. Our friend, Jack Mulvey, had become a deacon in the Catholic Church. Jack had given a great deal of his time to the Brady Center for the homeless and the less fortunate, so they had given a big banquet and awards dinner in his honor and also for some other devotees who had given their time to the church and charities.

We had a mutual friend, Dr. Ronald Burke, a professor at Syracuse University who also had been quite active in the church. We looked around for our good friend and, being unable to locate him, I asked Jack where Ron was. Jack said that Ron told him that he wasn't coming as he doesn't believe in the Lord. I said that I was truly sorry to hear that. I went back to our table and told Lore that Jack had told me that Ron isn't here because he doesn't believe in the Lord. Lore went to Jack's wife and told her that she was sorry to hear about Dr. Burke. Pat asked, "What about him?" Lore again repeated what I had told her. Pat said, "Ron isn't coming because he doesn't believe in awards." I went out and bought a set of hearing aids.

NINE

The Maverick

The adjective maverick: unconventional;
refusing to be bound by normal procedures.

I have been called a maverick at times. Normal procedures, I suppose, would be to get a job and stick with it forever, regardless. I held several jobs over the years; some interesting, some boring, some that showed promise and some that were strictly dead-end. Sometimes I quit my job. Sometimes I got fired. Sometimes I wouldn't be bound by normal procedures. Sometimes I tried to inject a little humor on the job. Sometimes I went too far. Sometimes I worked hard. Sometimes I hardly worked.

After high school, I found working in an office was low pay and very monotonous. Factory work paid more, but it, too, had no real future and also could get quite wearisome working eight and nine hours every night, doing the same thing over and over again.

In 1955, I started selling cookware part time. By 1965, I was selling cookware full time. For the next 25 years, I had cookware in my blood. I worked both as a salesman and sales manager.

Most people remember me as the "**cookware man.**"

However

I didn't always sell cookware.

I sold baby high chairs.
I sold encyclopedias. (part & full time for 10 years)
I sold stereo's and stereo music for Reader's Digest.
I sold candy to fund raising groups.
I sold children's magazines.
I sold Bibles.
I sold advertising.
I sold cable television.
I sold greeting cards to stores.
I sold uniform rentals etc.
I sold cosmetics, toys, ice cream, store signs.
I sold life and health insurance.
I sold industrial brushes.
I sold brushes to homes.
I sold janitorial and cleaning supplies.
I sold specialty chemicals.
I sold appliances at a Woolworth Store.
I sold baked goods at Sampson Air Base (3 years)
I sold bread and baked goods in the home. (4 years)

I sold bread and baked goods wholesale to stores.
I sold household products door to door.
I worked in a cheese factory (2 years)
I bottled milk.
I delivered milk to homes and stores.
I set type for books in a book bindery.
I worked as a radio repairman for General Electric.
I worked in a newspaper office. (4 years)
Bagged groceries and stocked shelves in a supermarket. (part time 3 yrears)
I managed two separate appliance stores.
I worked as a bill collector for a furniture store.
I worked as a bill collector for a TV cable company. (4 years)
I canvassed door to door for different companies and many different products.
I worked a wholesale business selling carded items etc.
I even preached a few sermons for my father-in-law in: New Berlin, NY—Lake Placid, NY—Ithaca, NY—Horseheads, NY—Valois, NY

I did not have a dull and boring life. I might have been a maverick. When things became dull and boring, I found something else to do.

My grandfather, my great grandfather, and it is my understanding that several great grandfathers back were all satisfied with making a living working 365 days a year doing the same thing over and over and over again. Milking and feeding cows, cleaning the barn, planting the crops, harvesting the crops, pitching the hay .... This life was not for Grandpa Ray.

TEN

Into Each Life

Every family looses part of the family as time moves on and our family is no exception. God has been very benevolent to us and we have had only limited tragedies. It's only right that I cover the sadness along with the rest. It is most fortunate that only a small amount of space is required to do this. It was only normal that my Grandparents passed away in their older years, as that is to be expected of all of us someday, but it is the young that we loose that breaks our hearts.

On March 18, 1949 my sister, Pauline and her husband, Victor Parker, had a baby boy that they named Victor, Jr. We called him Chipper. He was a beautiful blond and loving little boy. The Parkers had another boy and a girl by the end of 1952. Then tragedy struck. On January 19, 1953 Chipper fell into the Susquehanna river and drowned. It took several days to recover his little body and the family was heartbroken. The picture in the newspaper, of his father out in a boat with rescue workers looking for his son, still torments me. It was one of the saddest times that I can recall. We all loved this little guy more than words could ever express. Even as I write this, over 48 years later, the tears return and I weep some as memories come flooding back. Nothing is sadder or more devastating.

My sister, Barbara, and her husband, Joseph Rufo, lost their 17 year old son, Anthony, in April of 1980 from injuries caused by a motorcycle accident. Tony loved his motorcycle. We hadn't watched Tony grow up as he and his family lived in Florida and we seldom got together.

Lore and I were in Florida the year before his death. None of the family were able to make the trip to Florida for his funeral, but our hearts all went out to the Rufo family and only by the Grace of God and their trust in Him have they been able to withstand this tragic loss.

The following April (1981) we received word that my oldest sister, Vesta, had passed away in California. None of the family could get to her funeral. When my father heard that his first born was dead, he put on his jacket and went for his usual morning walk. He was gone for a very prolonged period of time and we became quite concerned about him. When he did return he said nothing, but he was stooped and notably grief stricken. He was never really the same again. My mother was suffering with terminal cancer and one of their children was gone.

The morning of December 5, 1981 my sister, Dorotha called me to tell me that "Dad passed away this morning with a heart attack." I went to Edmeston to be with my mother, and to help make final arrangements. He had died just the way that his mother had died 26 years earlier. He was sitting in his favorite chair talking to my mother. He let out a little gasp and he was gone. The funeral was on a cold, snowy day and it was a small group that came to say good-bye, as the family was well scattered around the country and most of his friends were already gone.

My mother, suffered with cancer a great deal in the last days of her life and on February 17, 1982 she passed away in the Cooperstown Hospital. We had her funeral on February 20, 1982. This was by far the hardest day of my life. After the funeral, I went to the coffin to say goodbye and to take my last look at the mother who had been so dear to us all. I found it difficult to leave the casket knowing that she wouldn't be here to offer that special smile, or the warmth that was ever present, even when she was suffering. **This woman was special.** Your parents can tell you how she could radiate love and always show her undying devotion to her children and grandchildren. You could sense her love, and she always understood.

I shall always miss that beautiful woman and to her memory I dedicate this little book.

I offer this little book to you to read whenever you might want to know a little about the family and your roots and some history of the 20th century.

In "Grandpa's Book," you may notice some mistakes. I never could figure out where to put my commas, my colons, my semicolons, or my apostrophes. I was never exemplary in English. I have always had problems with my: nouns, pronouns, adjectives, verbs, adverbs, prepositions, conjunctions and interjections, spelling and my English Teacher. Most of my mistakes have been corrected. My former English teacher, Mrs. Miner helped me to proof read my book as did our good friend, Rose Phillips. I called Millie Miner, and told her that I had finally finished the composition that she asked me to write in 1949 and told her that she would have to correct it and grade me. I still am picking on that woman after 50 years. This time she didn't send me to the office. She only said that she wished that I had applied myself 50 years ago as I have with this book. She enjoyed the book very much. I hope that you do too.

My hope is that you will overlook the mistakes and my shortcomings, both in my writings and in my life and accept this and me for what I have meant to convey: **"My love for my family!"**

I have ended this book on a sad note, but I would like you all to come together on my 100th birthday, January 1, 2032 and read, "Grandpa's Book."

Come, if you will, to the home for old people on my 100th birthday and read it to me. I will enjoy seeing and being with all of my loved ones. Bring your children and your grandchildren. If, by chance, God feels the need for an obstinate old salesman, desiring my company before that time, please gather together and read this catalogue of events of the past century and learn how we survived, how we lived and how we loved.

If I am not with you on that day and my ashes have been scattered on my mother's grave or buried between my parents, I want you to remember: My children, my grandchildren and my great grandchildren are very important to me....

I may have been a maverick. I may not have always been there for you, when you or your parents needed me. I, no doubt, have disappointed many people in my life and have fallen short of numerous, if not most, of my goals. I have not fallen short of the one main goal in life, and that goal is to have a wonderful, beautiful and loving family.

Your Grandfather loves each and everyone of you very much. Each of you are very dear to my heart, and I am as proud of each of you as I have always been proud of your parents, my children.

May God Bless You All...

Grandpa Ray

FROM GRANDPA SAMUEL TO GRANDPA RAY

GRANDPA SAMUEL TO GRANDPA RAY
DR. SAMUEL FULLER of the MAYFLOWER

Information regarding the FULLER GENEALOGY can be found in the "Genealogy of Some Descendants of Dr. Samuel Fuller of the Mayflower." by William Hyslop Fuller, 1910 [a copy may be found at the Onondaga County Library located at 447 S. Salina St., Syracuse, NY 13202]. Additional information can be found in *"FAMILIES OF THE PILGRIMS."* This book was compiled by Hubert Kinney Shaw, in accordance with research findings of George Ernest Bowman, founder and first secretary of the Massachusetts Society of Mayflower Descendants. This book was published by The Massachusetts Society of Mayflower Descendants, 9 Walnut St., Boston, MA in 1955. It includes the Mayflower Compact and information on most [if not all] of the original pilgrims. According to this book, SAMUEL FULLER was the 8th signer of the Mayflower Compact.

SAMUEL FULLER (1580-1633)

Samuel Fuller was the son of Robert Fuller, born in Redenhall Parish in Harleston, Norfolk County, England and baptized there 29 January, 1580. He died in 1633 at Plymouth, in New England. He married (1) Alice Glascock

(2) Agnes Carpenter (24 April 1613) who died in 1615 in Leyden, Holland; (3) Bridget Lee (27 May 1617) at Leyden.

Samuel Fuller was one of the band of Pilgrims who escaped from England in 1608 and settled in Leyden, Holland, in 1609. As the widower of Alice Glascock, it is recorded he was betrothed to Agnes Carpenter, 15 march, 1613, witnesses being her father, Alexander, Edward Southworth, William White, Roger Nelson, her sister, Alice and his sister Susanna (Fuller) White.

Later Samuel lived in Pieterskerkof, and after marrying Bridget Lee, took up residence near Marepoort. He joined with Isaac Allerton, William Bradford and Edward Winslow in a letter, 10 June, 1620, concerning the affairs of the Pilgrims, to their associates, John Carver and Robert Cushman, then in England. The record of his second and third marriage appear in "The Mayflower Descendants." Volume 8, p. 129 et seq.

The Pilgrims left Holland for America about Aug. 1, 1620 by way of Southampton, England, and Samuel Fuller's name appears as one of the signers of the "Compact" drawn up for the government of the Colony at Cape Cod, in November, 1620 in the vicinity of what is now Provincetown, MA. Some days later the Pilgrims made a permanent landing and settled at what is now Plymouth, MA.

Bridget (Lee) Fuller, the third wife of Samuel, came to America in 1623 on the *Ann*. The date and place of her death are not recorded, but it was after 1 March, 1664. In 1663 the town of Rehoboth voted to invite Mrs. Bridget Fuller to "come and dwell amongst us, to attend on the office of a midwife, to answer the town's necessity, which at present is great.

Samuel Fuller was a physician, and the biographical sketches published mention him as eminent in his profession, devoutly pious, and wise in counsel in the affairs of the Massachusetts Bay Colony. His will indicates that he was just, kind hearted and benevolent.

The children of:
DR. SAMUEL FULLER

1. A child that died in Holland
2. A child born in Holland that died young in Plymouth, MA
3. **SAMUEL,** born about 1625, m. Elizabeth Brewster
4. Mary, b____, m. Ralph James

SAMUEL FULLER

(Samuel), b.____,1625, in Plymouth, MA. His burial place was on the "Hill" at Plymouth, and the gravestone inscription reads: "Here leys yea bode of yea Rev. Samuel Fuller, who departed this life Aug. yea 17, 1695, in yea 71st year of his age. He was yea 1st minister of yea church in Middleborough.

He married Elizabeth Browser (Records 1st Church of Middleborough, (MA), who died in Plymton, MA, Nov 11, 1713. (Plympton Records).

Samuel Fuller was one of the 26 original proprietors of Middleborough. The Indians burned his home there in 1676 and he returned to Plymouth until the war with them was over. He had been educated for the ministry and preached several years at Middleborough, but was not ordained until 1694. His biographers describe him as a sober, grave, industrious, enlightened, and self-denying man.

His Children

1. Mercy, b. about 1656
2. Samuel, b. about 1659
3. Experience b. about 1661
4. John, b. 1663
5. Elizabeth, b. 1666
6. Hannah, b. 1668
7. **ISAAC**, b. 1675; m. Mary Prattt

ISAAC FULLER

(Samuel, Samuel), b. about 1675 in Plymouth, MA; d. 1727 in Brockton, (formerly N. Bridgewater, MA); m. Oct 20, 1709, Mary Pratt, married by Mr. Isaac Cushman (Plympton Records). He was a celebrated physician and resided at Halifax, MA. The first two children are recorded at Plympton and the others at Middleboro, MA.

His Children

1. Reliance, b. Dec. 28, 1710
2. Isaac, b. Sept. 24, 1712
3. Elizabeth, b. July 23, 1715
4. **SAMUEL,** b. Jan 28, 1718/19 m. Elizabeth Thompson

5. Micah, b. Jan. 31, 1719/20

6. Jabez, b. May 7, 1723

7. Mary, b. Aug.23, 1726

SAMUEL

(Isaac, Samuel, Samuel), b. Jan. 28, 1718, at Halifax, MA; date of death not found; m. Sept. 30, 1743, Elizabeth Thompson, b. Aug. 7. 1726; a descendant of John Thompson of Plymouth, MA. The first three children recorded in Halifax, MA.

His Children

1. **ZADOCK,** b. Sept. 19, 1744; m. Alice Porter

2. Elizabeth, b. Dec. 28, 1745

3. John, b. march 30, 1748

4. Lemuel, b. _____

5. Samuel, b. _____

ZADOCK FULLER

(Samuel, Isaac, Samuel, Samuel), b. Sept. 19, 1744; d. Sept. 17, 1818, in Lanesboro, MA; m. Dec. 3, 1767, Alice Porter, "Both of Halifax, MA" She d. in Lanesboro, Oct. 26, 1830, aged 84.

Zadock Fuller was a soldier in the Revolutionary War.

His Children

1. Sarah, b. Sept. 27, 1768

2. Elsie, b. Feb. -, 1771

3. Jabez, b. Jan 27, 1773

4. Abigail, b. March 4, 1777

5. Samuel, b. Sept. 27, 1779

6. Zadock, b. Feb. 4, 1781

7. **NOAH**, b. April, 9, 1787 m. Lois Goodrich

NOAH FULLER

(Zadock, Samuel, Isaac, Samuel, Samuel), b. April 9, 1787; d. Oct. 8, 1866, in Lanesboro, MA; m. Lois Goodrich, b. Aug. 25, 1791, d. Oct. 26, 1846 in Lanesboro. All children were born in Lanesboro, MA.

His Children

1. Eliza, b. Feb. 6, 1809

2. Lucy Ann, b. Jan. 27, 1811

3. **THOMAS ROYCE**, b. April 6, 1813; m. 1. Harriet M. Goodrich; m. 2. Sarah Backus

4. Laura Ann, b. Aug. 27, 1816

5. Adah M., b. Jan. 3, 1819

6. Huldah M., b. March 11, 1821

7. Ruth, b. March 29, 1823

8. Charlotte, b. April 4, 1825

9. A son. b. Oct. 25, 1827; d. Nov 17, 1827

10.Charles Hiram, b. June 26, 1829

11. David Porter, b. Oct. 25, 1831

THOMAS ROYCE FULLER

(Noah, Zadock, Samuel, Isaac, Samuel, Samuel), b. April 6, 1813, in Lanesboro, MA; d. March 30, 1891 at Edmeston, NY; m. 1. Feb. 5, 1837, Harriet M. Goodrich, b. Dec. 15, 1816 in New Berlin, NY, d. there Oct. 13, 1843; m. 2. Dec. 25, 1844, Sarah Backus, b. April 27, 1826, in New Berlin, NY, d. March 26, 1896 in Edmeston, NY.

He moved to Pittsfield, Otsego Co., NY then in 1848 to Watson, Lewis Co., NY. In 1867 he went back to Pittsfield and then in 1885 to Edmeston, NY.

His Children

1. **THOMAS WESLEY**, b. May 12, 1838; m. Alvira T. Morton.
2. Zadock I., b. Aug 8, 1841
3. Ruth M., b. Aug. 16, 1846
4. Child, b. Dec 29, 1848; died young.
5. Heman N., b. April 22, 1850
6. Charles H., b. June 19, 1852
7. Warren B., b. Aug. 30, 1855
8. Lois Elmira, b. Oct. 28, 1860
9. Eva May, b. Nov. 23, 1863

THOMAS WESLEY FULLER

(Thomas Royce, Noah, Zadock, Samuel, Isaac, Samuel, Samuel), b. May 12, 1838 in New Berlin, NY; d. Dec. 30, 1890; m. Oct. 22, 1858, Alvira T. Morton, b. May 6, 1838.

His Children

1. Charles Wesley, b. May 18, 1860
2. **THOMAS LEANDER**, b. Sept. 7, 1862; d. Aug. 21, 1940
3. Frederick H., b. June 20, 1876 in Pittsfield, NY
4. Floyd Z., b. Dec. 1879 in Pittsfield, NY

THOMAS LEANDER FULLER

(Thomas W., Thomas R., Noah, Zadock, Samuel, Isaac, Samuel, Samuel), b. Sept. 7, 1862, in Pittsfield, NY; d. Aug. 21, 1940 in Edmeston, NY; m. Vesta Green, b. April 6, 1872, in Glenfield, NY; d. April 20, 1955 in Edmeston, NY. Both are buried in Schribners Cemetery, New Berlin, NY.

His Children

1. Bessia Louisa, b. May 23, 1893; d. April 12, 1979; m. Elbert A. Rood Children: 1. Ethel 2. Irene 3. Stuart

2. Flossie Mai, b. Oct 3, 1895; d. Jan. 4, 1903 [in Lowville, NY]

3. **CLARENCE EUGENE**, b. June 24, 1897; d. Dec. 5, 1981 in Edmeston, NY. m. Vera A. Welch, d. Fe b. 17, 1982.

CLARENCE EUGENE FULLER

(Thomas L., Thomas W., Thomas R., Noah, Zadock, Samuel, Isaac, Samuel, Samuel) b. June 24, 1897; d. Dec. 5, 1981[funeral 12/8/81] in Edmeston, NY; m. Sept. 5, 1917, Vera A. Welch; b. May 16, 1899, d. Feb. 17, 1982 [funeral 2/20/82] in Edmeston, NY both buried at Union Cemetery in Edmeston, NY Otsego Co.

Children of:
Clarence and Vera Fuller

1. Vesta Elizabeth, b. Oct. 15, 1918; d.April 9, 1981 in California.

2. Dorotha Mae, b. May 8, 1921

3. Robert Leander, b. Aug. 26, 1922

4. Beatrice Cora, b. July 26, 1924

5. Pauline Ruth, b. April 17, 1929

6. **RAYMOND CLARENCE**, b. Jan. 1, 1932

7. Barbara Jean, b. Feb. 5, 1935

THE FULLER SIBLINGS

VESTA ELIZABETH, b. Oct. 15, 1918, d. April 9, 1981 in California; m. June 25, 1938 in Edmeston, NY to Russell Ripley; b. May 1, 1917

Children:1. Male child died at birth, June 23, 1939   (buried   in Homer, NY)

DOROTHA MAE, b. May 8, 1921, m. May 29, 1948 in Edmeston, NY to Harold Mort; b. Oct. 26, 1912; d. June 24, 1985 (buried in Rochester, NY)

Children:

1. Darlene Dixie, b. May 15, 1950

2. Donna Marie, b. Aug. 8, 1951

ROBERT L., b. Aug. 26, 1922, m. Feb. 11, 1943 to Elsie Maas. b. Sept. 29, 1921at Little Church Around the Corner in NYC

Children:

1. Robert L. Jr., b. Sept. 8, 1943

2.Patricia Anne, b. Sept. 25, 1947

BEATRICE CORA, b. July 26, 1924, m. Feb. 15, 1943 in Edmeston to Bernard Willis Ritchey, b. Jan. 30, 1922

Children:

1. Karen Louise, b. Oct. 29, 1946

2. Bernadine Lou, b. Oct. 23, 1947

3. Raye Ellen, b. May 19, 1949

4. James Clinton, b. May 3, 1950

5. Allen Douglas, b. Oct. 17, 1951

6. Theodore Weldon, b Jan. 30, 1953

7. Kirt Bernard, b. April 23, 1955

PAULINE RUTH, b. April 17, 1929; m. Oct. 25, 1947 in Edmeston, NY to Victor Parker, b. Oct. 25, 1929

Children:

1. Victor Lee, Jr., b. March 18, 1949. Drowned, Jan. 19, 1953, buried in Union Cemetery, Edmeston, NY

2. Richard Lynn, b. Nov. 10, 1951

3. Deborah Kay, b. Dec. 9,1952

4. Bonnie Jo, b. Dec. 20, 1954

5. Doreen Jill, b. April 19, 1956

6. Mark Rodney, b. Sept. 7, 1960

RAYMOND CLARENCE…see below

BARBARA JEAN, b. Feb. 5, 1935; m. April 17, 1954 in Edmeston to Joseph Rufo, b. Jan. 7, 1933

Children:

1. Victoria, b. Feb. 8, 1955

2.Valerie, b. Nov. 25, 1956

3. Joseph, Jr., b. Sept. 3, 1960

4. Anthony, b. Dec. 2, 1963, d. April, 1980 in Florida [motorcycle accident].

RAYMOND CLARENCE FULLER,

(Clarence E., Thomas L., Thomas W., Thomas R., Noah, Zadock, Samuel, Isaac, Samuel, Samuel), b. Jan. 1, 1932 in Edmeston, NY; m. in New Berlin, NY, 12/25/50; (1.) Mary Jane Chase, b. Nov. 28, 1934 in Ithaca, NY, divorced: 11/18/74 in Syracuse, NY. (2.) Eleonora Anna Lohninger Davies in Edmeston, NY on 2/2/85, b. 12/14/37 in Austria.

CHILDREN OF RAYMOND FULLER
& MARY JANE CHASE FULLER

1. Raymond Clarence, Jr.; b. Oct. 13, 1951; m. Maxine Fuller, 8/20/71

2. Jacqueline Elizabeth b. Nov 19, 1952; m. William Young, 12/28/74

3. Terri Lee; b. Feb. 23, 1955; m. Lynn Gaiteri, 8/17/74

4. Penny Sue b. May 2, 1957; m. Carlos Benedict, 7/4/81

5. Pamela Jo b. Apr. 22, 1958 m. (1.) David Goldberg (2.) Robert Hickman, 7/3/93

6. Thomas William; b. Mar. 16, 1960; m. Sallie Cubie 7/18/81

CHILDREN OF:
RAYMOND CLARENCE FULLER, JR. & MAXINE FULLER FULLER

1. Matthew Raymond Fuller;   b. Aug. 12, 1975 m. Amy Lynn Clayton on May 28, 1994

   1. *Rachel Nicole b. Sept. 28,1994*

2. David Kenneth; b. Jan. 18, 1977 m. Ann Munchel on July 11,1998

3. Katherine (Kate) Elizabeth;   b. Jan. 8, 1981

JACQUELINE ELIZABETH FULLER [WILLIAM YOUNG]

1. Elizabeth Marie; b. Feb. 5, 1988

2. Christopher Tomas; b. Nov.23, 1992

TERRI LEE FULLER [LYNN JAMES GAITERI]

1. Lee James; b. Nov. 18, 1976

2. Katrina Joy; b. Aug. 18, 1978,

m. Jason Manning on June 5, 1998

PENNY SUE FULLER [CARLOS BENEDICT]

1. Jessica Lynn; b. April 7, 1982
2. Jonathan Michael; b. May 7, 1984
3. Rebecca Marie; b. Nov. 9, 1987
4. Samuel Carlos; b. July 10, 1995
5. Caleb Joseph; b. Aug. 22, 1997

PAMELA JO FULLER [ROBERT HICKMAN]

1. David Goldberg, Jr. b. Sept. 27, 1983
2. Dominic Hickman; b. Nov. 8, 1990

THOMAS WILLIAM FULLER & SALLIE CUBIE FULLER

1. Thomas Leander; b. Dec. 17, 1987
2. James Robert; b. Sept. 22, 1989
3. William Frances; b. April 22, 1991
4. Grace Ann; b. May 8, 1993

Printed in the United States
23584LVS00001B/46-66

9 780595 199570